TREASURE ISLANDS
A Guide to the British Virgin Islands

By Larry and Reba Shepard

MACMILLAN
CARIBBEAN

First published 1989

Published by *Macmillan Publishers Ltd*
London and Basingstoke
Associated companies and representatives in Accra,
Auckland, Delhi, Dublin, Gaborone, Hamburg, Harare,
Hong Kong, Kuala Lumpur, Lagos, Manzini, Melbourne,
Mexico City, Nairobi, New York, Singapore, Tokyo

ISBN 0-333-46022-7

Printed Hong Kong

British Library Cataloguing in Publication Data
Shepard, Larry
  Treasure islands: a guide to the British
  Virgin Islands.
  1. British Virgin Islands. Visitors' guides
  I. Title   II. Shepard, Reba
  917.297'2504

ISBN 0-333-46022-7

Cover photograph published by
courtesy of Anne Bolt.

Contents

Dedication

To those wonderful, friendly people
the residents of the
British Virgin Islands
who have
made our stay here
so very enjoyable.
We are proud to call these islands — 'Home'.

Larry and Reba Shepard
Yacht *Borne Free*

Introduction

A personal message from the authors

The British Virgin Islands are quiet and peaceful, almost like an oasis that time has passed by. When asked about our island home, we answer, 'The island of St Thomas in the U.S. Virgins has more than 50,000 people living on that one island. The British Virgin Islands has only about 11,000 people on all of their seven populated islands — and it makes a whale of a difference.'

The atmosphere is less frenzied and frantic, more relaxed and friendly, and there are all the popular tourist attractions that visitors to tropical islands expect — with fewer people sharing them. We have white and pink sand beaches; clear, azure waters, blue skies, colourful flowering trees and shrubs; delightful scenery both above and below the water; protected seas and coves for yachting — all served by modern tourist facilities.

Nowhere in all these Caribbean islands are the people more friendly, nor is the crime rate lower than here. All this makes it not only a great place to live, but a great place to visit. This has been our home for more than seven years, and we love it more each and every day that we spend here.

Larry and Reba Shepard
Sailing Yacht *Borne Free*
Road Town, Tortola

1 Location and Geography

Extending south-east from the Florida Keys in a semi-circular arc to Trinidad in South America are the islands of the Caribbean. Looking on the map like irregularly spaced garden stepping-stones, they make an almost continuous chain which loosely connects North with South America, enclosing the tropical waters of the Caribbean Sea.

The first long stride along this chain is from Florida to Cuba, the largest island of the group; then a smaller stride to the storied island of Hispaniola, which contains both Haiti and the Dominican Republic. The third step, now due east, is to Puerto Rico, a territory of the United States. These three islands were originally Spanish possessions, their 'Pearls of the Antilles', known as the Greater Antilles.

The chain of islands east of Puerto Rico is known as the Leeward Islands of the Lesser Antilles, and a short step east, about 70 miles from Puerto Rico, brings us to the first of this group — the Virgin Islands. This name has long been used by both historians and mariners for the group of islands that lie between Virgin Passage (about 65° W) and Anegada Passage (about 64° W). Resting on a submarine plateau whose axis runs east-west along 18° 25′ N for about 70 miles, this island group is comprised of about a hundred small islands and cays.

Viewed together, the Virgin Islands present a dramatic appearance, with rugged hills rising abruptly from the blue-green sea, the slopes covered in most cases with trees and

Paradise found   (*Larry and Reba Shepard*)

1

British Virgin Islands

Existing National Parks

1 Sage Mountain (1964)
2 Botanic Gardens (1979)
3 Queen Elizabeth II Park (1974)
4 Mt. Healthy, Windmill Ruin (1983)
5 Rhone Marine Park (1980)
5b Rhone's Anchor (1980)
6 Virgin Gorda Peak (1974)

7 Little Fort (1978)
8 Spring Bay & The Crawl (1969)
9 The Baths (1987)
10 Devil's Bay (1969)
11 Fallen Jerusalem (1974)
12 West Dog (1974)

Proposed Protected Areas

13 Muskmellon Bay, Guana Island
14 Cam Bay, Great Camanoe
15 Area of Anegada/Horseshoe Reef
16 North Sound
17 The Dogs
18 The Baths Area

19 The Tobagos
20 The Bight, Norman Island
21 Sandy Cay
22 Fat Hog's Bay, Tortola
23 Areas on Beef Island
24 Sage Mt. Watershed

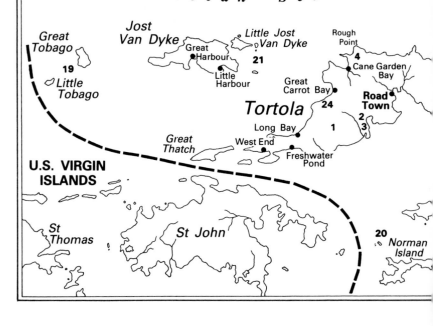

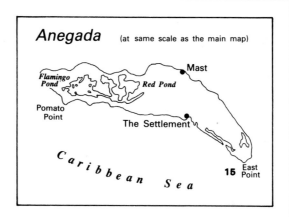

Anegada (at same scale as the main map)

Flamingo Pond
Mast
Red Pond
Pomato Point
The Settlement
15 East Point

C a r i b b e a n   S e a

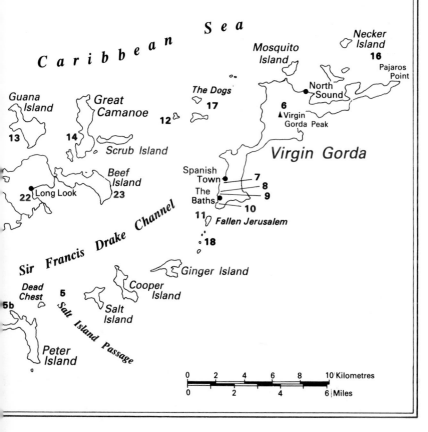

S e a

C a r i b b e a n

Necker Island
16
Pajaros Point

Mosquito Island

North Sound

Guana Island

Great Camanoe

The Dogs
17

6
▲Virgin Gorda Peak

13   **14**   **12**

Scrub Island

Virgin Gorda

Beef Island
23

Spanish Town
7
8
The Baths
9
10

22 Long Look

11 Fallen Jerusalem

18

Sir Francis Drake Channel

Ginger Island

Dead Chest
5

Cooper Island

5b

Salt Island

Peter Island

Salt Island Passage

| 0 | 2 | 4 | 6 | 8 | 10 Kilometres |
| 0 | | 2 | | 4 | 6 Miles |

undergrowth, while the deep valleys open invitingly. Like the edges of roughly torn pages, the irregular coastline creates myriad small bays and coves, many with golden sand beaches, which makes an attractive meeting of land and water.

The general appearance is that of a partly submerged mountain range, the higher peaks forming the chief islands, while the lesser flanking peaks form the smaller, outlying islands. The one exception to this volcanic structure is the island of Anegada, a coral atoll at the north-eastern edge of the group.

Although geographically a unit, the Virgin Islands became politically separated early in their history as pawns in the rivalries between warring European powers. The group was discovered by Columbus during his second voyage in 1493. He named them after St Ursula and her 11,000 virgins.

The original inhabitants were Indians but in 1555 Emperor Charles V of Spain sent forces that invaded the islands, defeated the Caribs, claimed the territory, and ordered the annihilation of the natives.

The Spaniards called them 'useless islands' and, for a century, the islands were considered too small and unimportant for

From Peter Island looking towards Dead Chest with Virgin Gorda, the 'Fat Virgin' lying on her back, in the distance   (*G. W. Lennox*)

settlement, remaining without permanent inhabitants. Because of this and their proximity to the sea lanes between Europe and the larger Spanish islands of the Greater Antilles, during the sixteenth and early seventeenth centuries they were chiefly in the hands of buccaneers, who used them as a base to launch their attacks on Spanish vessels.

In 1585, between Christmas and New Year's Day, Sir Francis Drake sailed through the channel between the islands that today carries his name, on his way to attack the Spaniards at Puerto Rico. On his last voyage in 1595 Drake anchored near 'the lland called the Virginies in a great bay between 2 llandes'. This 'very good rode, had it beene for a 1000 sails' must have been Virgin Gorda Sound at Virgin Gorda, which was reached on 8 November.

It is believed that Columbus may have named the largest island Tortola — Spanish for the turtle dove — but another account states that early Spanish settlers on Virgin Gorda may have given Tortola its name. Two of the other large islands, Anegada and Virgin Gorda, also have Spanish names. Virgin Gorda, the 'Fat Virgin', was probably so named since the island's profile as seen from the deck of a boat in Sir Francis Drake Channel is that of a fat woman lying on her back. Some of the other island names come from the early buccaneer days, such as Norman Island after a French pirate, Thatch Island after Edward Thatch (or Teach — commonly known as Blackbeard) and Jost Van Dyke possibly from a Dutch privateer or early Dutch settler of that name.

Although the islands were claimed by England as early as 1628, the Dutch were the first true settlers, arriving in St Croix in 1643, and at Soper's Hole at the west end of Tortola in 1648 — the Tortola settlement being used by freebooters and privateers. The Danes colonised St Thomas and St John in 1672. The English captured Tortola and the eastern islands from the Dutch in 1672, but they did not consolidate their position there until 1680.

From this point on, the islands were divided politically into two groups. The western group, comprising the principal islands of St Thomas, St John and St Croix, was ultimately consolidated under the Danes. In 1917 Denmark sold her holdings to the United States, and today these are the United States Virgin Islands.

The eastern group, comprising the principal islands of Jost Van Dyke, Tortola, Peter, Virgin Gorda and Anegada was consolidated under the English, and today are known as the British Virgin Islands.

Climate and Weather

The islands lie within the trade wind belt and possess a pleasant sub-tropical climate, with temperatures that vary only a few degrees during the year. Daytime winter temperatures average about 82° Fahrenheit (28° Celsius), with summer temperatures only slightly higher at 86°F (30°C). Sea breezes temper the occasional hot summer day, and there is a moderate fall of about 10°F (6°C) at night. An average year-round temperature of 78°F (26°C) provides a nearly perfect climate, which is one of the British Virgin Islands' chief assets.

Because of the almost constant temperature, the seasons are determined by rainfall, and the year is divided into wet and dry seasons, rather than warm and cold. Here also the seasonal changes are moderate, as most of the rain is in the form of showers — widespread continuous rain is rare. Showers occur

A rain-shower makes its way towards the islands   (*B.V.I. Tourist Board*)

The crystal-clear waters of Gun Creek and Virgin Gorda Sound, from a vantage point on Virgin Gorda Peak   (*B.V.I. Tourist Board*)

all year round, the difference being that in the dry season (February through April) showers are mainly light, while in the wet season (May through November) they may be heavy. As in all tropical climates, the showers start and end suddenly, and the water quickly evaporates. So even if you are caught out in a shower, you're soon dry again. The average rainfall in the B.V.I. is less than 35 inches annually.

Around the islands, the trade wind blows from the east with a high degree of constancy throughout the year and, to a large extent, offsets any adverse effects of high temperature or high humidity. Winds average from 10 to 15 knots, dropping to about 8 knots in the fall, but rarely blowing more strongly. Sometimes in December and January wind velocities may get up to 20–25 knots; these are known locally as the 'Christmas winds'. Trade winds bring the small, white puffy clouds called 'fair-weather cumulus', so attractive to photographers. Fog is practically unknown.

This region is liable to be affected by hurricanes, but these tropical storms are infrequent in these islands, averaging about four in a century. If a hurricane should happen, except on rare occasions its occurrence is limited to the late summer and fall. Hurricanes can be devastating, but current technology provides the ability to track their course with great accuracy, allowing those in the possible path time to take precautions. This has substantially reduced the effect of these violent storms.

The average water temperature of the sea that surrounds the islands varies little with the seasons. During the winter the lowest is about 76°F (25°C); the highest is about 85°F (30°C) in the fall. The average rise and fall of the tide is only about one foot, and in the open waters tidal currents are almost non-existent, rarely exceeding a knot or two even in the restricted channels between islands. For the most part, there is little difference between the air temperature and the water temperature, and when you combine this with the crystal clarity of the water, it makes swimming, snorkelling, and scuba-diving a delight.

2 The British Virgin Islands

There are about 40 islands, rocks and cays that make up the British Virgin Islands. With the exception of Anegada, all are 'high' islands of ancient volcanic origin. The entire island group contains a total of 59 square miles. The islands are situated on a relatively shallow undersea bank, where the water depths average less than 200 feet, and most of the islands surround Sir Francis Drake Channel, which has average depths of from 30 to 60 feet. All the islands except Anegada are formed of fragmented volcanic rock and highly contorted sediments into which metals have been intruded. There is a thin

The late afternoon light illumines the north shore of Tortola, looking towards three peaks on her west end, reminders of ancient volcanoes (*B.V.I. Tourist Board*)

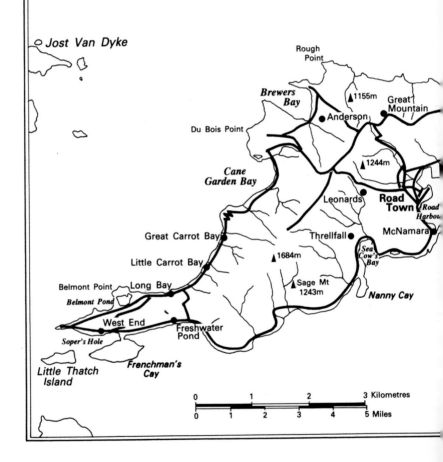

Tortola

C a r i b b e a n   S e a

Jost Van Dyke

Rough
Point

Brewers
Bay

▲1155m   Great
Mountain

Anderson

Du Bois Point

Cane
Garden Bay

▲1244m

Leonards   Road
Town   *Road
Harbou*

Great Carrot Bay

Threllfall   McNamara

*Sea
Cow's
Bay*

Little Carrot Bay

▲1684m

Belmont Point   Long Bay

▲Sage Mt
1243m   *Nanny Cay*

Belmont Pond

West End   Freshwater
Pond

Soper's Hole

Little Thatch
Island   *Frenchman's
Cay*

0		1		2		3 Kilometres
0	1	2	3	4		5 Miles

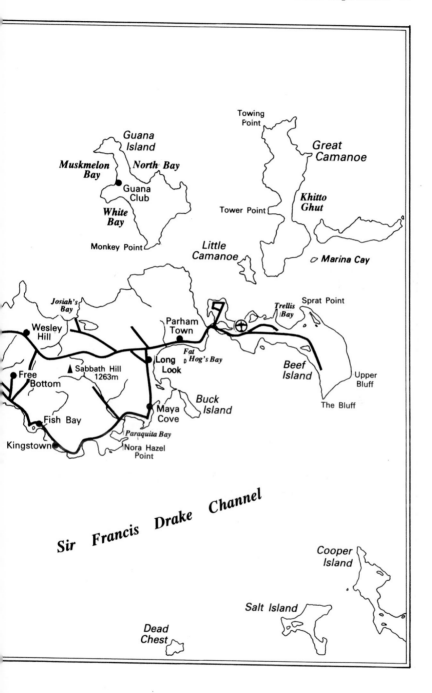

The rain forest, Mount Sage, Tortola   (B.V.I. Tourist Board)

overlay of loam soil which supports vegetation. There are no signs of recent activity, such as sulphur or hot springs.

Anegada, the northern and easternmost island of the group, in contrast to its neighbours is a low coralline island, barely 30 feet high. It has no rocks like the other islands, but is a recently uplifted coral island consisting entirely of limestone. Anegada has very little soil, limestone outcrops are extensive, and there is very little surface fresh water, though there are a number of fresh-water wells, believed to be accumulated rain-water in the limestone layers.

Although there are over 40 islands in the group, many of them are small cays and rocks. Seven of the larger islands are inhabited; here is a brief introduction to 11 of the principal ones.

Tortola

Tortola, the largest island, is roughly 15 miles long and 3 miles wide, running almost due east-west along the north side of Sir Francis Drake Channel. It is composed of a long chain of hills which are uninterrupted by any transverse valley or pass. It is usually impossible to cross from shore to shore without ascend-

The main square, Road Town, Tortola   (*Michael Bourne*)

ing some 1,200 feet as its rugged hills rise abruptly on all sides from the coast. At the western end of Tortola, there are several inverted cone-shaped mountains that are reminiscent of volcanoes. Tortola is also the highest island; Mount Sage rises to an elevation of 1,780 feet. This island contains the only rain forest in the group.

Road Town, the Territory's capital and principal city, is centred on the south coast of Tortola, adjacent to Road Harbour, the principal commercial port for the islands. Tortola is the most heavily populated island, with over 9,000 people in 1985. In addition to the capital city, there are smaller settlements at West End, Long Look and Cane Garden Bay, the latter being one of the most beautiful of the island bays. Road Town is the centre of political and economic activity in the islands, containing many shops, offices, hotels and other commercial enterprises.

Virgin Gorda

Virgin Gorda, the second largest island, is also the second highest, Gorda Peak rising to 1,359 feet. The island lies eight

Huge boulders lie helter-skelter at The Baths of Virgin Gorda. Their origin is an unexplained mystery   (*Michael Bourne*)

miles north-east of Tortola and has a population of about 1,500. It is ten miles long, of irregular width and shape, Gorda Peak being the dominant feature at the centre of the island. This peak throws off a lateral ridge to form a long narrow peninsula on the north-eastern side composed of irregular rugged hills terminating at Pajaros Point in a remarkable pinnacle rock, 120 feet high.

This tongue of land, when combined with the surrounding barrier reefs and islands to the north, creates Virgin Gorda Sound, also known as North Sound, a large sheltered bay that is a hub for marine-related activity and the site of several resort hotels.

The part of the island that lies south of Gorda Peak is called The Valley, and is relatively flat. Here is located the main settlement of Spanish Town, which in its early history was the capital of the island group. Both a yacht harbour and an air strip in The Valley near Spanish Town provide a means of access to and from the other islands of the group.

South of Spanish Town toward the south-western end of the island is Virgin Gorda's most striking feature. Here the land has been broken up by some violent action of nature into immense blocks of igneous rock, closely allied to granite, which are scattered about the coast. These enormous boulders coming to the water's edge at a spectacular beach have created lovely pools called The Baths, a major tourist attraction.

Quartz as well as small quantities of mineral ores such as copper, gold, and molybdenum are also found on this part of the island, and the remains of a crude smelter can be found there from copper mining operations in the nineteenth century.

The cays and islets south-west of Virgin Gorda as far as Round Rock, about two miles off, are almost all composed of granite; in fact, Fallen Jerusalem, the largest of them, is so named from its resemblance to a town in ruins.

Ginger Island

Heading south-east from Virgin Gorda, and along the south side of Sir Francis Drake Channel, the first large island is

Ginger Island — a lonely, uninhabited island that is rarely visited because it has no safe, comfortable anchorage. A small lighthouse at the top of the island peak provides a navigational aid to mariners seeking the entrance to Sir Francis Drake Channel from the east.

Cooper Island

Next is Cooper Island, with an anchorage at Manchineel Bay on its north-east coast. Here are a few vacation homes and a small beach bar and restaurant that has long been a favourite among yachtsmen, and the recent placement of moorings has made this a safe overnight stop. At the north end of the island, about at water line, is a rock formation that looks much like the British Lion.

Manchineel Bay, Cooper Island　(*B.V.I. Tourist Board*)

Borne Free at anchor off the beach at Salt Island — Tortola in the background   (*Larry and Reba Shepard*)

Salt Island

Salt Island, west of Cooper, has one of the friendliest settlements in the islands. The population today rarely exceeds four to five people, but back in 1845 it was as high as one hundred. The people of Salt Island exist by gathering salt from the two ponds near the village, by fishing, and by selling souvenirs to visitors. The salt ponds are owned by the Queen, and the islanders pay a nominal annual fee to the Sovereign to harvest the salt here.

Off the point south of the village lies the famous wreck of the Royal Mail Steamer *Rhone*. Three hundred and ten feet long and forty feet wide, the *Rhone* was launched on 11 February 1865 in Southampton, England, a member of the Royal Mail Steam Packet Company which carried cargo and mail from England to South America. On 29 October 1867, she was struck by a hurricane and driven on to the rocks at Salt Island, where she broke up and sank in from 40 to 90 feet of water. Some of the *Rhone*'s ill-fated passengers are buried on Salt Island.

The skeleton of the broken hull can easily be seen from the surface in the clear waters, and her coral-encrusted superstructure is now home to an enormous variety of marine life. This wreck has been described by *Skin Diver Magazine* as the 'Queen of the Caribbean Wrecks', and is a renowned and beautiful site for diving and snorkelling.

Peter Island

Peter Island is the next in the chain of islands along the south side of Sir Francis Drake Channel; it lies almost due south of Road Harbour on Tortola, eight miles across the channel. A few fishermen, and the staff and guests of an exclusive resort hotel make up the inhabitants of this lovely island. It has one of the most beautiful beaches in the Caribbean at Deadman's Bay on its north-east corner; other anchorages on both sides of the island provide safe haven with quiet and seclusion.

Peter Island's quiet, secluded beach on Deadman's Bay, one of the world's most beautiful beaches   (G. W. Lennox)

Norman Island

The last island in the chain that lies along the south side of Sir Francis Drake Channel, and the most south-westerly island of the group, Norman Island is uninhabited and haunted by its many legends. There is a tradition that this island is the model for Robert Louis Stevenson's *Treasure Island* and, while the geography of the island fails to match the geography in the book exactly, the history of piracy on this island is strong.

One of the safest and most secluded anchorages in all the islands is here in a bay called 'The Bight'. Close by on Treasure Point are two large caves at the water line where treasure is said to have been found. This is one of the islands' most popular anchorages.

Jost Van Dyke

This island, which at one time in its history had a colony of Quakers, lies north-west of Tortola. Today there are two small settlements, one at Great Harbour and one at Little Harbour, the island's principal anchorages. The residents mostly provide services to the many charter vessels that call here. Great Harbour is a port of entry with a relaxed atmosphere. It is also the site of Foxy's (an island character) annual Wooden Boat Regatta. Just east of this island is Sandy Cay, a small coral islet that has one of the most beautiful elkhorn coral reefs in all of the Caribbean.

Guana Island

Lying off the north-east coast of Tortola, this is one of the few privately owned islands of the group. It is operated as a private club, and the accommodations on the island are open only to its guests. Just to the east of this island lie the islands of Great Camanoe and Scrub, both of them occupied by a few private homes. They are rarely visited by tourists.

The Queen Elizabeth II Memorial Bridge, a narrow one-lane structure which connects Tortola and Beef Island   (*Larry and Reba Shepard*)

Beef Island

So named because at one time it was exclusively a rangeland for beef cattle, Beef Island is separated from the east end of Tortola by a narrow channel. Connected to Tortola by a bridge not much longer than its name — The Queen Elizabeth II Memorial Bridge — it now holds the island group's principal airport and one of its two links by air to the rest of the world, the other link being the airstrip on Virgin Gorda. Off the end of the airport runway on Beef Island is Trellis Bay — a sheltered anchorage with a fine beach. Close by, across the channel to the north, lies Marina Cay, a small islet with a beautiful beach, and a small hotel and restaurant.

Anegada Island

Anegada comes from the Spanish word for sunken land; its highest point is only 28 feet above sea-level. It lies about 15 miles north of Virgin Gorda and is so low that it is not visible from a boat until it is close upon it. As an additional hazard to sailors there is a twenty-mile reef called Horsehoe Reef surrounding Anegada, with only one good anchorage at the west end.

There are over 65 known wrecks around the island, ranging from sixteenth century treasure ships to a modern-day cargo vessel — making this island a skin-diver's heaven. During the pirate era, Anegada was a pirate hangout because of its reefs and difficult access. Not only did it provide seclusion, but it offered a steady supply of ships to loot as they were wrecked on the reef. Today, the island is inhabited by about one hundred people; there are an airstrip, two restaurants and a small hotel, mostly frequented by fishermen and visiting yachtsmen.

3 Transportation Services

Getting there

No guidebook is really complete without a section on 'How to Get There', and since the British Virgin Islands are small, lightly populated islands, much of whose charm comes from their quiet seclusion, getting there takes a little more planning than flying into a country with a major jet airport or two. Both the principal B.V.I. airport on Beef Island and the airstrip on Virgin Gorda accommodate only propeller or prop-jet planes,

Air B.V.I.'s local service at Beef Island, one of the four airlines which connect the B.V.I. to the rest of the world   (G. W. Lennox)

not jets, and therefore the traveller from North America or Europe must plan at least a two-leg flight: one from their home base to a major jet airport in the Caribbean, and then a connecting commuter plane flight to the B.V.I.

The major international jet airport closest to the B.V.I. is at San Juan, Puerto Rico, only about 120 miles — 45 minutes flying time — to B.V.I. airports on Beef Island and Virgin Gorda. San Juan airport is serviced by many of the world's major airlines.

There are several U.S. and Canadian airlines that offer daily flights from the North American continent to San Juan, Puerto Rico. Service to and from South America is not as frequent, but connections can be made to most major South American cities. From Europe there is a direct, but not daily, service to San Juan from London, Frankfurt and Madrid.

From San Juan airport it is easy: in 1988 there were four commuter airlines offering frequent non-stop services between San Juan and both the Beef Island and Virgin Gorda airports. Two of these were commuter links operated by major U.S. airlines serving San Juan airport. Of the others, one is based in the B.V.I., the other in the U.S.V.I.

If you are coming from the U.K., there is an alternative route via Antigua in the Eastern Caribbean. In 1988 there was a direct, but not daily, service from London to Antigua. The direct commuter flight from Antigua to the B.V.I. takes only ninety minutes, a scenic trip over the tops of islands all the way. When coming from this direction, a little more advance planning is called for, since service schedules are seasonal, and not all flights operate daily.

Seasoned travellers recognise that where a change of carrier occurs on a long trip, not often but sometimes the checked-in baggage does not arrive with the traveller. It is recommended that luggage be checked on the initial leg only to the jet terminal in the Caribbean, such as San Juan. Pick the luggage up there and then personally re-check it with the commuter connection to the B.V.I. Just in case, pack a toilet kit, swim suit, and any necessary medications or other personal items in a 'carry-on' case, and wear clothing on the flight which is suitable for tropical climates — and have a change of clothing with you.

On arrival, the traveller will find modern terminal facilities at both Beef Island and Virgin Gorda, and immigration and customs officials whose main concern is to get the visitor through as quickly and painlessly as possible.

With proper planning, it is possible to get to the B.V.I. today from almost any place in North or South America or Europe on the same day you leave. We've come a long way since Columbus.

Travel between the U.S.V.I. and the B.V.I.

Some visitors, especially those from the U.S.A., choose to split their time between the two island groups, and spend some time in each. Because of their proximity and close historical ties, there is a great deal of travel between the two island groups, both by visitors and island inhabitants. As a result, transportation facilities are well-developed, frequent, and fast.

There are three ways to make this trip — by plane, by seaplane, and by ferry boat.

Commuter flights by plane between St Thomas airport and

Road Town ferry dock and customs office, and one of the islands' ferry boats which ply between the B.V.I. and the U.S.V.I. (*Michael Bourne*)

Beef Island and Virgin Gorda airports in the B.V.I. are both fast and frequent. It is a short flight at a relatively low altitude, which offers an unequalled opportunity to view both the island groups from the air.

The V.I. seaplane shuttle is one of the few remaining scheduled seaplane services in the world. These amphibious planes take off and land on the water, then taxi up on to shore pads where passengers are embarked and disembarked. It is a unique experience. The seaplane shuttle operates between the islands of St Croix and St Thomas in the U.S.V.I. and Tortola in the B.V.I. The service to Tortola comes into a shore pad at West End, adjacent to both the customs and immigration building and the ferry dock. In 1988, the service to Tortola was three times a week.

Ferry boats are the form of transportation most used by the residents, as well as many visitors, to get from one island group to the other. Services connecting Tortola and Virgin Gorda in the B.V.I. with St Thomas and St John in the U.S.V.I. are both numerous and reliable. The trip from the ferry dock at Tortola's West End to the ferry dock on the waterfront in

Small boats are easily available for hire   (*B.V.I. Tourist Board*)

Charlotte Amalie harbour in St Thomas takes only an hour. Travel time from the ferry docks in both Road Harbour and Virgin Gorda is only slightly longer. A daily service is also provided between West End on Tortola and Cruz Bay on St John, with a travel time of about half an hour.

It is possible to take an early morning ferry from Tortola or Virgin Gorda to St Thomas, spend the day shopping or as you please, and then return on a late afternoon ferry to the B.V.I. The ferry service runs in daylight hours only — there is no service at night. The ferries run frequently and it is usually not necessary to book seats in advance.

Inter-island services within the B.V.I.

There is scheduled service by air between the three airports in the B.V.I. on Beef Island, Virgin Gorda, and Anegada. The shuttle plane service between Beef Island and Virgin Gorda is daily, and frequent. Service to Anegada is not as frequent — in 1988 it operated twice a day, four days a week.

The principal inter-island ferry service plies between the ferry dock near Spanish Town on Virgin Gorda, and the dock in Road Harbour on Tortola. A frequent daily shuttle service is provided at a modest cost. The trip takes about forty minutes.

The Peter Island Hotel operates a private ferry service from Road Harbour to Peter Island for its visitors and guests, with several daily ferries. Many of the other hotels and restaurants on outlying islands also provide a private boat service for their guests on request.

In 1988 the North Sound Express inaugurated a thrice daily ferry service between Trellis Bay on Beef Island and The Bitter End on North Sound, with flag stops at Leverick Bay and Biras Creek. A connecting bus at Trellis Bay extends the service to Beef Island airport and Road Town.

Schedules and fares of both airlines and ferries are subject to periodic change. Specific and up-to-date information may be obtained from the B.V.I. Tourist Board, or may be found in *The Welcome Tourist Guide*, a bi-monthly magazine published in the islands, available at most tourist facilities.

Private charters

There are a number of licensed air charter carriers throughout the Caribbean islands which can arrange special flights by plane or helicopter. There are also private boats available for charter both to islands within and outside the B.V.I. Term boat charters are one of the major tourist industries in the B.V.I., and are given special coverage in Chapters 10 and 11.

Ground transportation

Public roads in the B.V.I. are mostly limited to the two largest islands of Tortola and Virgin Gorda. Anegada and Jost Van Dyke have a few miles of public roads, and Peter Island has a few miles of private roads.

The visitor arriving by air will find both individual and group transportation available at the airport. These are in the form of taxis, and a vehicle unique to the islands, the safari van. This is an open-air vehicle, with an awning over six rows of bench-like seats behind the driver's cab. It can carry up to 30 people at a

A private road cut into the hillside on Peter Island. Deadman's Bay is in the foreground   (*Michael Bourne*)

time. The safari vans not only meet flights at the airport, but meet the island ferries at the docks, and by grouping passengers on these vehicles can provide transportation at lower cost than the private taxi. Many of the island hotels contract with the safari van drivers to meet incoming guests. A taxi service, either private or shared, is available almost everywhere that roads exist, and the drivers, in addition to being skilful, are both friendly and helpful.

There are a number of rental car agencies on both Tortola and Virgin Gorda. They follow the procedures standard in most countries of requiring both a major credit card and a valid driver's licence from the visitor's country of origin. They will issue the required temporary B.V.I. driver's licence for a fee of $10.00. Because of the climate, open air vehicles such as Land Rovers and Mini-Mokes are available and popular.

Visitors to the B.V.I. from the heavily populated areas of North America and Europe will find that driving a vehicle here is very different, and in some ways much more interesting. For one thing, it is a pleasant surprise to find that there is not a single traffic light in all the islands! There are no expressways, either. On the contrary, because of the mountainous terrain, many of the roads are narrow, winding, and steep — a constant challenge to the driver's alertness and skill. Many rural parts of the islands are unfenced, and farm animals are permitted to graze freely. Take care — it is not unusual to round a curve and find a herd of goats or cows, or an occasional mule crossing the road. Driving here, as should be expected in a British territory, is on the left, and there are traffic circles where roads intersect, as is the practice in the U.K.

4 Public Services

Language

The language of the islands is English — but most of the inhabitants also speak a dialect called Calypso among themselves. While this dialect is based on English, it is usually incomprehensible to the off-island visitor.

Legal and judicial

The law of the Territory is made up of both the common law of

A policeman on duty   (*B.V.I. Tourist Board*)

Britain and statutory law — legislation enacted by the elected
Legislative Council. It is administered by the West Indies
Associated States Supreme Court, courts of summary juris-
diction, and magistrates' courts. The principal law officer is the
islands' Attorney General.

Police

The Royal Virgin Islands Police Force comprises the islands'
protective service. Highly trained and smartly uniformed, the
police enforce the laws of the islands courteously but firmly.
The Force maintains three stations in Tortola and one in
Virgin Gorda. These islands are remarkably crime free, with
one of the lowest crime rates in the Caribbean. It is the policy
of the government to keep it that way. A particularly hard line
is taken on drugs. The possession, distribution, or sale of drugs
is a felony, punishable by a stiff fine and detention in the
islands' not-too-pleasant detention facility, H. M. Prison, reputed to be the oldest building in Road Town still in use.

Customs

Import duties All visitors to the islands are required to clear
through customs upon entry. Visitors may bring any quantity of
personal belongings, food or drink into the islands for their own
temporary use without duty, but all true imports are subject to
duty, and the rate varies. Expensive personal items may also be
brought into the islands duty free on a non-permanent basis,
but a good-faith bond may be requested as an assurance that the
items are not actually being imported.

Yachts, both private and charter Captains bringing yachts
into the islands must clear into one of the ports of entry and
pay the required entry fee, including a charge for the length of
stay. There is a limit to the time a vessel not registered in the
B.V.I. may remain in island waters. Additionally, every person
on a charter yacht, whether a B.V.I. based yacht or a foreign
one, is required to pay a daily permit fee, called a cruising

permit, which is in lieu of the hotel tax payable while staying on the islands. Rates vary with the season, and are lower for B.V.I. registered yachts than yachts from other countries. Recently enacted legislation requires the licensing of non-B.V.I. based charter boats that operate in B.V.I. waters.

Ports of entry, where there are both customs and immigration personnel, and where vessels may clear both in and out of the country, are located at:

Great Harbour, Jost Van Dyke
Ferry Dock, Soper's Hole, West End, Tortola
Ferry Dock, Road Harbour, Road Town, Tortola
Virgin Gorda Yacht Harbour, Virgin Gorda
Nanny Cay Marina, Nanny Cay, Tortola

Immigration

Entering All persons entering the islands must clear through the Immigration Department. Visiting Canadian and U.S. citizens must produce either a Canadian or U.S. passport or a birth certificate or voter's registration card. Visitors from other countries must produce a passport. Vacationers are usually granted up to one month's stay. Longer visits must be cleared with the Immigration Department in Road Town, and may require return (or onward) transportation tickets; evidence of the ability to support themselves during their stay; and arrangements for accommodation.

Leaving There is a departure tax, payable when leaving the islands. Those leaving by air pay $5.00 at the airport; those leaving by private or charter boat pay $3.00 at the time the boat leaves the islands.

Animals Pets or animals may be brought in only after a permit has been secured from the local agricultural officer, and a health certificate is secured from a registered veterinarian. Pets will not be admitted without advance clearance.

Public health

The British Virgin Islands has good medical facilities, both public and private. The Peebles Hospital, named after its founder Major H. W. Peebles, was opened in 1921, and is centrally located in Road Town. Partially destroyed in the

A donkey-ride for two   (*B.V.I. Tourist Board*)

hurricane of 1924, it was rebuilt around the remnants of the pre-hurricane structure.

The medical department at Peebles Hospital maintains a daily out-patient clinic, and provides a weekly clinic on both Jost Van Dyke and Anegada. There is also a branch clinic on Virgin Gorda. The public health clinic provides health examinations, immunisations, pediatric care and a family planning service; there is also an emergency service. The hospital and its clinics are staffed by a chief medical officer, five doctors on Tortola, and one doctor on Virgin Gorda. There are also a number of physicians in private practice in the islands.

Public utilities

Electricity Electricity on all the islands is 110 volts, 60 cycles, which is compatible with North American practice, rather than the European practice of 220 volts. Power on the main islands is supplied by the Department of Electricity through a central generating plant which is reasonably reliable, but since there is no back-up plant, occasional interruptions of service may be encountered.

There was a time, not many years ago, when the islands' budget did not provide for twenty-four-hour operation of the electrical generators. At ten p.m. each night all the lights on the island went out when the generator was shut down, and did not go on again until morning. Today twenty-four-hour service is provided. On the outlying islands, power is frequently supplied by a private generator, especially in some of the larger resort hotels.

Gas There is no natural gas on the islands, and since heating is not necessary in the tropical climate, gas is usually used only as cooking fuel in larger installations such as hotels, where it becomes more economical than electricity. Cooking fuel is either butane or propane, imported into the islands by tanker and distributed in bottles to the end users. In recent years solar heat has become a principal source of energy for the heating of water.

Water Water is a semi-precious commodity in the B.V.I. While the islands receive rain all the year round, they are relatively small when compared to their neighbours, and the mountain peaks not as high, therefore they do not collect and retain as much water as on larger islands. There are no rivers or streams in the B.V.I. Islanders depend primarily on wells and collected rain water, through cisterns and small reservoirs.

Some of the larger hotels have installed desalinisation plants which make fresh water from sea water, supplementing the normal rainfall. The water supply is adequate for normal consumption, but water conservation is practised by all of the residents, and visitors are asked to do this too. Do not be surprised to find in your hotel room a reminder of the ways to conserve water.

Communications and radio The telephone service in the islands is provided by Cable & Wireless Ltd, a well-known British communications company. All of the inhabited islands are linked and receive a modern and reliable service. In addition to inter-island service, there is external cable, telex, and radio-telephone service to all parts of the world. Direct links

Though it is a low coralline island, there is fresh water to be found on Anegada about 4 feet below the surface. Several spots have been tapped for this fresh water source   (*Larry and Reba Shepard*)

are provided to the U.S.A., Canada, and the U.K.

The company also operates a maritime VHF radio station (Tortola Radio) on channel 27 which provides a service to vessels properly equipped with a licensed VHF marine transceiver. This service can link vessels to both the internal and international telephone systems.

There are no television stations in the B.V.I., but a cable TV distribution network enables subscribers to receive TV stations broadcasting from neighbouring islands as well as satellite stations broadcasting from North America.

Radio station ZBVI, a privately owned station, operates a 10,000 watt, 780 kcs transmitter on Tortola, providing local programming, news and weather to the islands.

Other services

Working Those who are considering entering the islands to live and work must contact the Labour Department. Working here is strictly controlled. Non-islanders may work in the islands only if they hold a valid work permit issued by the Labour Department for a fee, and they will secure work permits only where the position cannot be filled by British Virgin Islanders. Training is encouraged and often provided for local residents to fill key positions. The government requires that at least one-third of the work force for those receiving benefits under incentive legislation be island residents. However, in a group of islands with only about 11,000 people, many work permits are issued to non-islanders.

Residence To become a permanent resident, a certificate of residence must be applied for and secured from the government. There are a number of requirements that must be met, and information about these can be obtained from the Department of Immigration. There are a number of rights and privileges available to residents that are not available to visitors.

Buying land Land is available for sale or lease. There are two types — Crown land and private land. Crown land is rarely sold; however, very long lease arrangements may be available provided the investment made by the lessee seems favourable to the Territory. Private land may be sold outright or leased but, in both cases, the non-resident lessee or buyer must obtain a land-holding licence from the Department of Natural Resources and Public Health. There are fewer restrictions on land purchased for personal use than on land purchased for investment or development. Persons interested are usually well advised to consult with the appropriate governmental department or a registered agent on the island.

Investments The B.V.I. is a developing country, and investments are encouraged. Each type of investment has its own rules and regulations, and those interested should consult the appropriate government agency. For example, to own your own business a trade licence is required from the Department of Inland Revenue, as well as a work permit from the Department of Labour. The B.V.I. has no limitations on currency exchange, and potential investors should check their own country's exchange control regulations.

Taxes As in many developing countries, taxes are low to encourage investment. The tax base of the country is comprised of a personal income tax, a company or corporation tax, a property tax, and social security taxes if there are hired employees. There are no inheritance or capital gains taxes and no death duties. Full information on the islands' tax policy may be obtained from the Department of Inland Revenue.

Currency In 1967 the U.S. dollar was made the sole legal tender in the B.V.I. The close economic ties to the U.S.V.I. made this not only desirable, but necessary. First, large numbers of residents of the B.V.I. were and are employed in the U.S.V.I.; and second, the principal industry is tourism — the principal source of tourists being from the U.S.A. Making the dollar the legal currency in the B.V.I. made it much easier for everyone. Visitors from countries which have currency controls should ensure that drafts and travellers cheques are endorsed to facilitate cashing into U.S. dollars.

Postal system The Postal Administration functions as a separate department of the government. Besides the main post office in Road Town, there are two branch offices on Tortola, and one on Virgin Gorda. Sub-post offices will be found on several of the smaller inhabited islands. There are airmail links to St Thomas; to the U.S. and Canada through San Juan, Puerto Rico; and to Europe through Antigua.

The sale of special stamps issued for philatelists is an important function of the Postal Administration which provides a substantial source of revenue for the government. These special issues are both beautiful and unique. The B.V.I. is one of only two British territories that issue their stamps with the value of the stamp stated in U.S. currency. The other is Bermuda.

Education The Education Department is headed by a chief education officer who is the principal adviser on educational matters and is responsible for carrying out the educational policies of the government. Education is free and compulsory to

The main post office on Main Street in Road Town, Tortola
(*Michael Bourne*)

the extent that facilities exist. Primary schools are provided both by the government and local churches, and a high school provides secondary education with courses to G.C.E. 'A' level. Higher education is available at the University of the West Indies, with campuses on Jamaica, Barbados, and Trinidad. There are also several private schools in the islands recognised by the government. These are fee-paying, and primarily cater to kindergarten and pre-primary age groups.

Public holidays

New Year's Day (1 January)
Commonwealth Day (14 March)
Good Friday
Easter Monday
Whit Monday
The Sovereign's Official Birthday (2nd Saturday in June)
Territory Day (1 July)
Festival Days (3 days during the first week in August)
St Ursula's Day (the patron saint of the islands) (21 October)
Birthday of Heir to the Throne (14 November)
Christmas Day (25 December)
Boxing Day (26 December)

Finally, a word to the wise: the proximity of American neighbours whose holidays are different has an effect on many businesses in these islands. If you are in the British islands, for example, on the traditional American holiday for Independence Day, you may find some services closed.

5 The Land and Nature

Green hills rising steeply from white sand beaches are a typical
sight in the British Virgin Islands. The trees, vines, shrubs and
plants that make up the tropical covering become both the raw
material for many a native product and natural objects of
beauty, to be admired by all.

Old island stories tell of hundreds of ways to use nature's
bounty, and of knowledge gained and used when many islanders' lives depended upon the practical use of the wild vegetation around them. Some of this knowledge is in the fading
memories of the older generation and, unless recorded, may
become lost to those who follow. Happily, the present government cares about these traditions and, with cooperation and
support from all segments of the community, much effort is
being spent to preserve this cultural heritage.

There are trees which are used for boat building, vines for
basket weaving and fish traps, wood for carving, leaves and
fronds for weather protection of dwellings, sand and coral for
cement, clay for bricks, wood for charcoal, leaves and bark for a
variety of 'bush' medications, and fruits for island drinks. Many
plants are native to the islands, but some have been imported,
a few possibly early in history by the Indians who, it is believed,
brought in roots and seeds from other islands.

Island vegetation has great variety, even though much of it is
second growth. Most of the land was cleared years ago for sugar
and cotton cultivation during the plantation era. In some
places you will see arid land, marked by cactus, frangipani,
loblolly and wild tamarind; while in other places fruit trees,

flowers, and palms grow in profusion. Whether you see brown scrub or green vegetation on a hillside depends on the rainfall that part of the island receives. Everywhere along the seashore you find the sea grape, the mangrove, and the 'poison' apple tree — the manchineel. Some of the more common varieties of trees, plants, and flowers that visitors are likely to encounter are described on the following pages.

Fruit trees

Most of the common tropical fruit trees grow in the islands, and are usually found in backyard gardens, but some grow wild. To a resident, it is acceptable for their island neighbours to pick a fruit, even though growing in someone's yard. It is a charming tradition, never abused by the island citizens.

Both the dwarf variety of the common yellow dessert **banana** and the **plaintain** grow here, the latter used by the residents as a starchy fruit which is boiled, baked, or fried while under-ripe. The fruit of the **breadfruit** tree is also used as a starch in the local diet, baked, roasted, boiled, or french-fried. The **genip** tree produces a slightly sour marble-sized fruit that is very popular, and is eaten like a grape, while the local **lime** is small and juicy, and is served by local bartenders in season as an ingredient of mixed drinks.

Another tropical fruit is the **guava**, a yellow fruit that is used in juices, syrups, and even butter. The **mango**, a prolific fruit tree with pear shaped fruit, in season one tree can provide enough for a whole family. In addition to being delicious fresh, the mango can be used in chutney, nut bread, and ice cream. The elongated fruit of the **papaya** tree can be eaten raw when it is ripe, or can be boiled as a vegetable, pickled, or preserved while still green. The fruit contains an enzyme called papain, which is the chief ingredient in meat tenderisers.

The large green fruit of the **soursop** tree is a local favourite. The pulp is juicy, slightly sour, and is especially good in ice cream. The leaves, steeped in hot water, make a tea which is frequently used by residents for minor colds or illness. The **sugar apple**, also called **sweetsop**, produces a baseball-size fruit

with a sweet pulp, the consistency of custard. It can be eaten
fresh, or the green fruit can be boiled and eaten like potatoes
with steamed fish.

The **sea grape**, with its thick, rounded leaves and its large
drooping clusters of grape-like fruit is used in two ways. The
fruit can be made into a holiday wine or into a jam of excellent
flavour; the leaves are frequently used in the presentation of
other food as a green plate-liner. When presented along with
hibiscus blossoms, a truly tropical decor is created.

Other trees

There are many other varieties of trees found on the islands —
some can be put to a useful purpose, others are flowering trees
whose beauty supplements the already appealing landscape.
Here are some of the more common.

The **coconut palm** was introduced into tropical America by
the Spaniards, and is found today on most Caribbean islands. It
is frequently found fringing the many island beaches, where it
provides both shade and decoration. The fronds were formerly

A sea grape tree growing by the beach at Brewers Bay   (*Michael
Bourne*)

used in thatching, and even today are split for use in weaving hats, baskets and matting. Fresh coconuts have many uses — green coconuts containing coconut water can often be purchased from roadside vendors, while the mature nut can be eaten as it is, or grated and mixed with hot water to make the coconut milk which is used in many island dishes.

The **manchineel**, which is mostly found near the coastline, has an apple shaped fruit which is sometimes called 'the forbidden fruit from the garden of Eden'. It is potentially poisonous, and biting into it can cause your mouth to burn and your tongue to swell. Prolonged or excessive skin contact with its leaves can also cause irritation. A chilling tale is told in the islands of slaves who, wishing to do away with a particularly despicable master, inserted minute quantities of manchineel juice into an uncooked potato. Cooked, these small doses eventually proved fatal after being served to the victim over a period of time.

The **mangrove**, another tree growing along the shoreline, has numerous prop-roots that ultimately form an impenetrable mass. These roots play an important part in preventing erosion and in building land. The **portia** tree, also called the **maho** or **tulip tree**, grows on the shoreline, and its thick growth of heart-shaped leaves and colourful bell-shaped flowers are a welcome sight when planted on a barren shore. The straight-grained wood is cherished by boat-builders who make ribs and stems from the curved limbs.

The small yellow fruit of the **soapberry** tree contain a unique ingredient (saponin) which, when mixed with water, makes nature's own soap. The early islanders found that, when crushed and put into fresh water, the fruit produced plenty of suds. The dried seeds are used as marbles, seed jewellery, and even buttons.

The **tamarind** is not only an attractive flowering tree, but also has several uses. The red-striped yellow flower is used in dyes, the fruit has an acid pulp used in preserves, and the seeds can be cooked or ground into meal. Island lore says that switches used to beat slaves were cut from the tamarind.

One of the most beautiful sights in the islands is the **royal**

poinciana (also called the **flamboyant** or **flame tree**) in bloom. There are many of these trees in the B.V.I., and when the annual seasonal blooming occurs, the colourful masses of bright orange and red flowers make a spectacular flaming display everywhere.

Plants and flowers

The tropics are noted for the many varieties of plants and shrubs which grow in profusion, some having many uses, others

A flamboyant tree in full bloom outside the Treasure Isle Hotel   (*Larry and Reba Shepard*)

The century plant, often used on the islands as a Christmas tree
(G. W. *Lennox*)

adding colour and beauty to the countryside. The B.V.I. is no exception, and a description of a few of those that are found here follows.

The **century plant** is a tall, slender native succulent frequently seen standing out on the hillsides. It matures and flowers only once in many years (probably closer to ten than a hundred in spite of its name) and is then replaced by a new

The exotic looking turk's cap or barrel cactus   (*B.V.I. Tourist Board*)

plant growing out of the old. Islanders have found an original way to use the dead trunk and branches — when the blooms have dried up and blown away in the wind, the trunk is cut down, dried, and used in the islands as a Christmas tree.

Several varieties of cactus grow in the arid sections. Among them is the **turk's cap** or **barrel cactus** — as its name implies it is a deeply ridged barrel-shaped shrub whose red flowers protrude from the top like a cap, presenting a striking appearance. The **dildo cactus** is one of nature's cisterns, storing water in the tissue of its trunks and branches. Its pink flowers bear a sweet edible fruit.

Another succulent, both decorative and useful, is the **aloe**, whose thick, spiny-edged leaves exude a bitter, gelatine-like juice when cut. It has been used in the islands for many years to aid in healing burns and sores, and as a purgative and tonic. The fresh juice provides almost immediate relief when applied to sunburn, but care should be taken because it will also permanently stain fabrics. Aloe is used commercially as an ingredient in preparations sold by many pharmaceutical companies.

A plant with an edible root is the **elephant's ear**, whose tuberous root is called **taro** or **eddo**, a food staple in the tropics used much like a potato. In temperate zones it is considered an ornamental plant because of its large leaves.

Wild tantan grows almost everywhere in the brush, and is frequently considered a weed-like pest by gardeners. Yet it has a useful function, as the roots of this plant, through 'nitrogen fixing', enrich the soil. The plant's protein-rich leaves and pods are the sustaining diet of many of the islands' cattle and goats.

Among the many varieties of flowering plants are the **angel trumpet**, with its large and fragrant trumpet-like blossoms; the **canna lily**, with its scarlet flowers on long terminal stalks; the **frangipani** or **red jasmine**, with its fragrant waxy flowers from which perfume is made; and the **poinsettia**, whose scarlet petal-like leaves surrounding tiny yellow flowers are at their best around Christmas time.

Ginger thomas, a fairly large shrub with bright yellow bell-shaped flowers blooming in clusters, is frequently found growing along roadsides and along the base of fences throughout the islands. A description of the tropics would not be complete without the ever-present **hibiscus**, whose large, showy, colourful flower blooms only for a day. It is a favourite table decoration of the island chefs.

Among flowering vines may be found the **four o-clock**, whose blossom opens at four p.m. as the name implies; the **morning glory**, whose purple trumpet-like flower is familiar to all; and the spectacular **bougainvillaea**, whose brilliant red and purple flowers make a showy display over many an island fence or wall.

The hardy hiker, who is not afraid to tackle the trails up the slopes of Virgin Gorda peak, just might be lucky enough to find among the trees and shrubs that surround the trail one of the B.V.I.'s rare **wild orchids**.

Gardens with properly selected flowering plants display their blooms year-round in the tropical climate of the islands. There is never a season when a resident or visitor cannot pick a bouquet of fresh flowers for the table.

Birds

Experts estimate that there are eighty species of birds in these islands. There are land birds that nest in the hillside forests and brush, shore birds and waders that congregate in the shallow waters along the shorelines, and sea birds that can be seen flying over the open waters and nesting in the rocky peaks of the outlying cays. While many are local birds here all year around, some are winter migrants from North America, and others are members of wide-ranging oceanic populations. Birds are seen (and heard) everywhere and are a constant source of pleasure to all. Here are some of the more common species that are likely to be seen by the island visitor.

Land birds

In Columbus's account of his first voyage, he reported '. . .and the nightingale was singing, and other birds of a thousand

A selection of the beautiful B.V.I. stamps featuring the islands' birds.
Boatswain bird   Rain bird   Mocking-bird   Chinchary   Blue gaulin
Cowbird   Ground dove   Pond shakey   (*B.V.I. Philatelic Bureau*)

kinds, in the month of November there where I went.' In fact, somewhat more than 400 species of birds have been found in the West Indies, and the bird Columbus heard was later identified as the mockingbird, which is even today called a 'nightingale' in many Caribbean countries. In the B.V.I. the **northern mockingbird** sings its melodious phrases, especially in the winter months.

It is said that the island of Tortola was named for the turtle dove, and indeed one of the more common birds here today is the **zenaida dove**, locally called both the turtle dove and the mountain dove, whose mournful cooing is heard through the hills in the evening. Two cousins, the tiny **common ground dove** and the **bridled quail dove**, called the marmy dove, also nest in the undergrowth; while a second cousin, the handsome **red-necked pigeon**, is frequently seen in the flyways.

If a visitor watches closely among the many flowering shrubs, he is almost sure to see one of the islands' hummingbirds, moving back and forth and up and down with equal ease, feeding on the nectar in the blossoms. Two species of these tiny birds are found here, both in protective green colouring: the **green-throated carib**, and the **Antillean crested hummingbird**, with its conspicuous green crest. Two members of the cuckoo family also reside here, the **mangrove cuckoo**, known locally as the rain bird, and the glossy black **smooth-billed ani**, called the black witch by islanders.

Warblers are migrant winter transients in this region, and a member of this family who usually drops into the B.V.I. is the **yellow warbler**, which looks something like a canary, and is sometimes mistakenly called by that name. Less common, but occasionally seen are the **cape may warbler**, the **black-throated blue warbler**, and the **myrtle warbler**.

Only one of the finch family is common here — the small **black-faced grassquit**, sometimes called the parson bird for its dark dress; while two members of the flycatcher family are the aggressive **grey kingbird**, and the smaller, more retiring **Caribbean elaenia**. A predatory falcon seen soaring over the green hills is the **American kestrel** or **sparrow hawk**. Locally it is called the killy-killy from its shrill call. One of the more visible birds is a cousin of the mockingbird, the **pearly-eyed thrasher,** called the thrushee bird by the natives. This aggressive bird is frequently seen on and under the tables of outdoor restaurants, picking up pieces of fruit.

Seen everywhere in the open fields where cattle graze is the ubiquitous white **cattle egret,** locally called the cowbird. It looks like a small heron, and is in fact a member of that family, but it spends its time in the fields, frequently on the backs of the cattle with which it shares the field.

Finally, there is the official bird of the B.V.I., the friendly **bananaquit,** affectionately known as the sugar bird. It is a member of the honeycreeper family who feed on fruit, nectar and small insects. This small black and yellow bird is frequently found perched on an outdoor table, nipping into the sugar bowl in its constant quest to find something sweet.

Shore birds and waders

Along the island shores, among the sea grape, the manchineel and the tangled roots of the mangrove, are found the many shore birds of the islands. Some of these are quite shy, avoiding populated areas, and running for cover when humans approach. To find the more reclusive of these birds, the dedicated bird-watcher might consider visiting Paraquita Bay on the south shore of Tortola, a shallow, marshy bay almost completely enclosed by heavy mangrove growth, seldom visited by boats or humans. Here are some of the shore birds commonly found in the islands.

The heron family is well represented by three frequently seen species, the **little blue heron,** also called the blue gaulin, the **green heron,** or little gaulin, and the **yellow-crowned night heron,** or night gaulin, the latter being active in the daytime as well as at night, despite its name. The **stilt,** a graceful black and white bird with very long pink legs, is a native not only regularly seen, but whose noisy yapping is also frequently heard.

Plovers are quite common, and are winter transients. Visitors regularly seen are the **thick-billed plover;** the **black-bellied plover,** with its plaintive 'pee-a-wee'; the **killdeer,** named for its distinctive call; and the **ruddy turnstone.** Sandpipers are also transient, coming all the way from northern North America. Commonly found here in the winter are the **spotted sandpiper,** and both the **greater** and the **lesser yellowlegs.** Other species of these long-ranged travellers occasionally drop in.

If the birdwatching visitor is both patient and lucky, he might see the elusive, ghost-like **clapper rail** hiding in the mangrove roots, a bird more often heard than seen.

Sea birds

Soaring over the waters of the B.V.I. are a number of sea birds. Some of them are only passing through, but others breed in the rocky heights of the out-lying islands.

One of the most beautiful and easily recognised of the sea birds is the tropicbird. Two of the only three species of this widespread oceanic bird are found here — the **red-billed tropicbird,** and the **white-tailed tropicbird,** both known locally as the boatswain bird. Although they have different markings, both are easily recognised by their very long and narrow forked white tails. Another wide-ranging species that spends most of its time at sea, but nests here, is **Audubon's shearwater,** locally called the pimlico. Fishermen frequently see this low-flying bird well away from the islands.

Another bird commonly seen flying over the anchorages is the **royal tern.** This bold bird will not only swoop down to pick up food thrown into the sea, but if a visitor on a charter yacht holds out a biscuit or cracker, well away from the rigging, it will fly down and take the morsel right out of his hand. The tern is sometimes locally called a booby, but it should not be confused with the **brown booby,** also found here, which is a larger bird, more brown than white. Another cousin of the tern found here, and distinguished by its black head, is the **laughing gull,** the only gull likely to be seen in the West Indies.

The magnificent frigatebird's real name is just that — the **magnificent frigatebird.** This large bird, mostly black with a forked tail over three feet in length and with a proportionate wingspread, is usually seen soaring high over the sea around the islands. Like most of the sea birds it is a fish-eater, and one of its traits is to steal fish caught by other, smaller birds. It is a common sight to see the frigatebird swoop down on either a tern or a tropicbird that has caught a fish, and chase the smaller bird until it is forced to drop its catch. The frigatebird then spirals down and catches the morsel before it hits the water.

Then there is the ever-present **brown pelican**, a great favourite with visitors, here as everywhere. Although ponderous looking when perched on a post or the rail of a boat at anchor, it is extremely graceful in flight, skimming within inches of the water surface, then soaring up as high as thirty feet, folding its wings and plummeting like a dive-bomber in a spectacular plunge into the water. It might be considered absurd in appearance, with its huge flat bill and ponderous pouch, but its solemn appearance is belied by the twinkle in its eye, and its friendly, comical manner has made it appealing to all. It is even the subject of a well-known limerick:

A resting pelican   (*B.V.I. Tourist Board*)

A wonderful bird is the pelican,
His beak holds more than his belican.
He can take in his beak
Enough food for a week,
But I'm damned if I know how in helican!

The birds of the islands are everywhere and are enjoyed by all, whether a casual observer or an avid birdwatcher. The veteran birdwatcher should bring not only his binoculars but, to help in identification, should also consider securing and bringing a copy of James Bond's book, *Birds of the West Indies* (Houghton Mifflin Co., Boston, 1961), generally considered the most complete guide to the birds of these Caribbean islands. Bird lovers are also directed to a 1985 B.V.I. definitive stamp issue on 'Birds of the British Virgin Islands'.

Other fauna

Animals   There are virtually no wild four-legged animals in these islands; the single exception, and it is rare, is a squirrel. Some goats and cattle, as well as small horses roam freely on Anegada, and might be considered 'wild'. A few wild goats still inhabit Jost Van Dyke, and some wild cattle have been reported on uninhabited Norman Island. On the principal islands of Tortola and Virgin Gorda, large animals are all of the domesticated variety, principally cattle, goats, horses, and mules. Many of these wander about the islands freely, untethered and unfenced. So if a visitor sees a large four-legged animal coming out of the brush — not to worry, it will almost certainly be one of the domesticated species.

Reptiles   There are about half a dozen species of lizards on the islands, all of them harmless. Most are never seen, staying well hidden in the brush. One that is frequently seen by the visitor is the **man lizard**, a small harmless lizard under ten inches long, frequently seen climbing up walls. It is a greyish brown colour, which seems to change in different lights and backgrounds. It is sometimes incorrectly called a 'gecko'. This reptile feeds only on insects, and its antics are frequently comical.

A much larger lizard is the **iguana**, a nocturnal lizard which once thrived in these islands but is now quite scarce. Two have been seen recently in different locations on Peter Island, and some on Anegada. One lives in the rocks above the beach on Deadman's Bay, and can occasionally be seen in the afternoon on a warm rock, basking in the sun. The other lives near the top of the hills. They fear man and will run away when approached. Once a delicacy on the local dinner table, iguanas have been hunted to near extinction.

Insects While the B.V.I. has its normal share of insects of all kinds, these are not considered 'buggy' islands, primarily because of the relatively light rainfall and the constant trade winds. Almost all of the island restaurants and hotel dining rooms are open-air and unscreened, without any problems. Insects are not a pest here, being kept under reasonable control by the many island birds.

About the only unwelcome insect that will come to the attention of the visitor is the common mosquito. Although this insect can be found anywhere fresh water is allowed to stagnate,

The small harmless man lizard is frequently seen on the walls of houses   (*B.V.I. Tourist Board*)

it does not really become troublesome except after the occasional heavy showers, when they hatch and bolster the market for mosquito repellent. People in boats anchored offshore are seldom bothered.

An unusual insect is the tiny 'love bug' which lives under the portia or maho tree, its sole diet being that tree's fallen fruit; another is the frangipani moth which feeds only on frangipani leaves. It is believed that the moth and the frangipani are mutually beneficial to each other.

Note   The reader will understand, in a subject this broad, that not all flora and fauna can be included in the confines of a guide book; and in both this chapter and the chapter which follows, our coverage is limited to those species most likely to be encountered by the island visitor.

6 The Sea and Nature

The living coral reefs

From a hillside overlooking a bay, coral reefs appear as dark patches, giving no clue to the actual beauty they contain when explored in close proximity. A coral reef, while appearing to be a chain or ridge of rocks or range of sand — an inanimate object — is actually a cluster of a large variety of living organisms. The clear, warm waters in the British Virgin Islands support a diverse and intriguing complex of coral reefs: each

A delicate sea fan growing on the reef. When viewed by the snorkeller, it sways in the current of water surges   (*Caribbean Images Ltd*)

coral formation is different, colourful, and made up of many striking varieties, from the delicate **staghorn** to the stunning **pillar coral** growing in cathedral-like spires.

The **sea fans**, with their lacy leaves, add the blues, pale greens and lavenders, while the fuzzy skeletal formations called **corky sea fingers** are brown and resemble desert cactus.

While beautiful, these reefs are also important, since living, healthy, coral reefs are essential for the beaches as we know them — coral-sand beaches. Coral reefs also support a wide variety of sea life. Corals come in as many varieties as they do colours — from the hard corals to the most primitive of the multicellular animals on the reef, the **sponges**.

Sunlight and clear water are required to continue the growth of the coral, and reefs in water too deep to permit sunlight to penetrate soon die. Most corals are safe to touch, with one particular exception, the **fire coral**, which can cause an irritating rash when brushed.

Reefs attract snorkellers, who are fascinated by the variety and the beauty of the silent world beneath the sea, and especially that which is part of a coral reef: encrusted sponges that come in all shapes ranging from simple covering mats to great baskets and tubes, carpets of soft yellowish **colonial anemones**, and short-spined **redsea urchins**. There are also sturdy fan-shaped clumps of **elkhorn coral**, which dominate the shallow, high-wave zone on fringing reefs, and are often oriented in the direction of the incoming waves. Their close relative, a delicate and more easily broken branching coral known as **staghorn**, is found in areas where wave action is less, interspersed with encrusting **brain corals**, gorgonians such as **sea whips**, **sea-plumes** and **seafans**, and **fire coral** with its finger-like growth form.

Molluscs

In and among the reefs, in beds of seagrass, which is in itself a food-rich habitat for a number of animals, live molluscs, some friendly and some not. The **long-spined black sea urchin**, commonly seen in the islands, is a hazard to swimmers, and should be given a wide berth. The **queen conch**, the large edible mollusc whose heavy pink shell is a common item in curio shops, ranges through the grass beds to feed, sometimes burrowing completely under the sand in order to avoid a predator such as the **spiny lobster**, **sting ray** or **octopus**. Groups of adult queen conch may be found on the sandy, weedy, bottom as they move, seasonally, from bay to bay in search of food or places for reproduction.

Less prevalent is the **king helmet**, a feeder on sea urchins prized by collectors. Another edible mollusc, and a local favourite food, is the **West Indian topshell** (locally, whelk).

Divers admiring some of the different varieties of fish found in the waters of the British Virgin Islands   (*B.V.I. Tourist Board*)

Fish

Reefs also attract many species of fish, and over 200 species of marine fish from the Caribbean are known, each with its role in the life of the underwater world. Among them are the predatory **grouper**, the crab-eating **squirrel fishes**, and algae-grazing **surgeon fishes**.

The **angelfish** are friendly little seafarers in all shades of blue, yellow and green; one variety is called the queen because of the crown on its forehead; another, the grey angelfish because of its silver tones; and another, the French angelfish, is black with a sprinkling of yellow spots. No matter what their colouration, they all appear to be pouting.

This is not so with the long thin **trumpetfish**, nor with the **jewfish**, nor the **sea bass**, one of the giants of the reef, with many individual finny examples stretching to 8 feet and weighting 700 pounds. It seems natural that the **cardinal** fish should be clothed in bright red and have what appears to be a regal bearing.

The coral reef has its corps of professionals — surgeons,

The reef is home to several colourful varieties of angelfish
(*Caribbean Images Ltd*)

doctors, schoolmasters and sergeant majors, each doing its job with easy precision. The **schoolmaster**, part of the snapper family, is about two feet long and has a severe and dour countenance, while the **sergeant major**, sporting military-like chevrons on its flanks, is the most cheerful and approachable, and can often be fed out of a friendly snorkeller's hand.

Several brown stripes on a beige body mark the **doctorfish**, while the **ocean surgeon**, which varies in colour, has a circle of small blue lines around its eyes, giving the impression that it is wearing glasses.

Other reef fish which might be seen by a snorkeller could include a squadron of **squid** swimming backwards, butterflies, peacocks, parrots and squirrels. The **butterflyfish** is delicate and small, as its name implies, and has black stripes across its eyes, almost as if it was wearing patches. The **peacock**, a flatfish member of the flounder family, is beige with blue starlike spots and a colourful tail resembling the prancing peacock on shore.

The colourful **parrotfish**, whose bright green, red and yellow colours blend together as naturally as those of its feathered counterparts, is often seen swimming in schools, roaming over the shallow reefs. It is equipped with beak-like teeth that are perfect tools for scraping the furry crust of algae from dead coral. Much of the sand on local reefs is a by-product of this method of feeding. Good visibility in tropical waters may explain the evolution of bright colour patterns for sexual recognition.

The **squirrelfish**, with its prickly dorsal fins, looks like a spiny cactus as it swims, and the **spadefish** looks like a miniature zebra, with its silver and black stripes; the queens wear their crowns in many species. There are also jacks and kings; **amberjack, yellowjack,** and **kingfish** swim by the reefs occasionally, but are more often found in deeper waters, and are considered among the prize catches of sport fishermen.

No matter which reef you travel, you may well be met by a **grunt** (named from the sounds they seem to make) or by schools of **sunshine**, small golden members of the damselfish family. The larger species of common reef fish include the big-mouthed carnivorous **grouper**, ghostly platter-sized **angel-**

fish, and the secretive, heavy-bodied **moray eel** which is usually found where reefs are in deeper water.

Deep crevices and overhanging ledges are typical daytime dens of the **Carribean spiny lobster** which lacks the massive claws of its northern cold-water relative, and its darker cousin, the **spotted rock lobster** which has the peculiar habit of clinging upside down in a protected den. It is not likely that you

A fine specimen of the Caribbean spiny lobster (*Caribbean Images Ltd*)

will see a lobster in shallow water, as they are eagerly sought after by professional divers and fisherman as a delicacy.

Sea shells

There are many sea shells in the Caribbean region which are as beautiful and varied as other places in the world. Large and small shells of bright colours, varied patterns, shiny surfaces and fascinating sculpture abound. The casual stroller on a beach may only find fragments of shells or, if lucky, a freshly washed up specimen, unbroken and unfaded, truly a treasure.

Snorkelling the water that laps a beach with shell fragments can reveal shells in shallow as well as deeper water. Certain types of bottom, the beginner discovers, host different types of shells. **Helmets** and **conchs** favour turtle-grass areas, whereas **cone** shells and **cowries** favour the underside of rocks or hide in amongst coral. **Hermit crabs** crawl about wearing various kinds of shells for the collector's selection.

As shells in the waters are found it becomes apparent that they aren't like the shiny, beautiful specimens in the shell store. Live shells in the sea have a periostracum or 'skin' that clouds the colours and sculpture. Sometimes there are calcium deposits which also need to be removed so that the surface sculpture and delicate colours can be revealed.

There are many techniques which are used to collect shells and different underwater environments which play host to the numerous families of shells. In many parts of the country there are shell clubs where enthusiastic collectors gather to talk shells, organise field trips, exchange shells, or listen to mala- cologists, professionals in the field. This section on shells in the islands was written by Bruce Crystal, an avid collector and expert on shells of the Caribbean.

The visitor is reminded that living sea shells are protected in the Marine Parks of the B.V.I. and should not be removed, but left for others to see and enjoy. In the gift shops in the island hotels you will usually find some excellent books with colour photographs to help you identify the coral reef growth, the various reef fish, and the great variety of shells that may be

found in the waters of the Caribbean. Many of these stores also sell a handy waterproof plastic card with pictures of both fish and shells, which you can take with you, and which will help you enjoy the beautiful reefs of the B.V.I.

Whale migration

Humpback whales migrating from South America to Greenland are commonly sighted in the Anegada Passage from mid-February to mid-April. Whale watching has become an accepted sport; the forty foot average length of a humpback does attract attention as they make their way south each winter to breed. As soon as their calves are old enough to sustain the long journey, pods of whales begin migrating northward to summer feeding grounds in the Arctic Ocean.

Whale watching is controlled by the National Marine Fisheries Service (NMFS), which considers any activity that disturbs the normal pattern of life for the whales harassment — and harassment is illegal. Whales are extremely protective of their young, and even a spectator boat approaching too close can cause the mothers to swim in circles. Spectators who see a change in the activity pattern of the whales as they approach by boat should immediately withdraw.

Turtles

It is possible that a snorkeller or diver might encounter a young **hawksbill** or **green sea turtle**, or even a grey, heavy-bodied **nurse shark**. These are relatively benign creatures, that will ignore divers or snorkellers unless provoked.

The turtles are considered reptiles, and the green sea turtle has a greenish or olive-coloured shell, lives in warm seas, and lays highly nutritious eggs, and has meat that is much valued for food. The hawksbill is a carnivorous turtle which also lives in warm seas, and has a shell that is much valued for tortoise-

Snorkelling among the different corals in the warm, translucent waters of the B.V.I. is a pleasure many can enjoy   (*Caribbean Images Ltd*)

shell uses such as jewellery and decorative combs.

Turtles are a protected species in the British Virgin Islands, and tortoise shells are prohibited as imports into the U.S.A.

Game fish

While the snorkeller on the reef looks at all the fish, the sport fisherman takes his lot one at a time, and hefty and varied it can be. Lawrence Rockefeller, it is said, was responsible for promoting deep-sea sport fishing here in the 1960s, as a boon to the new resort he had built in the U.S. Virgin Islands.

The most sought after species is the **blue marlin**, a very large marlin, widely distributed in warm seas, which can be found at the outer edges of the relatively shallow underwater plateau that surrounds the Virgin Islands. Two other varieties of 'bill-fish', the **white marlin** and the **sailfish**, a relative of the sword-fish, are also caught in these waters.

Anegada is the **bone-fishing** capital of the B.V.I., where the fish are found in the reefs that surround that island. This is a sportsman's fish, as the fun is in the catching, rather than in the eating, even though they are edible.

Other sport fish prized by anglers are frequently found in the more shallow waters lying outside the perimeter islands. These include **dolphin fish** (dorado), **tuna**, **wahoo**, various **snappers** and **groupers** and **barracuda**. Most of these are edible, but some varieties may be subject to ciguatera toxic poisoning, depending on their size and where they are caught. A general rule is, if you are out fishing and catch a fish which you cannot identify as a ciguatera-free species, don't eat it.

7 National Parks and Protected Areas

With tourism as the principal foundation of the island economy, the B.V.I. government has long realised the need for
protection of their beautiful scenic areas. To meet this need,
the National Parks Trust was formed, which has the responsibility for management of natural terrestrial, marine and historic
resources in legally protected areas. It works closely with the
Ministry of Natural Resources and is funded largely by the
government. It also receives support from the Eastern Caribbean Natural Area Management Program (ECNAMP) funded
by the Jackson Hole Preserve Inc., a Rockefeller endowed fund.
With this help, current parks are maintained, critical areas
identified, and new parks are planned.

Because the marine environment is such an important part of
the ecosystem, as well as one of the most fragile parts, special
attention has been given to marine parks. These parks are open
to the public, but use of the areas is subject to some regulations
which concentrate on conservation of natural and historic resources, and protection of endangered or locally important
species. By setting aside these preserves, it is hoped that there
will not only be greater enjoyment by the public, but increasing
awareness of the necessity to protect these sensitive areas.

Visitors are expected to honour these conservation efforts,
because damage to the environment inevitably happens when a
high volume of tourists pass through. All are asked to help keep
damage to a minimum by following some basic rules:

1 Take only photographs, and leave only your footprints.

   a) Collecting any living creature, whether wildflower,

The fern house in the Botanical Gardens, Road Town,
Tortola   (*Michael Bourne*)

Colourful sponges are beautiful in their natural habitat, but smell
horrible if removed from the sea   (*Caribbean Images Ltd*)

shell-fish or coral, quickly depopulates an area; please leave them for others to enjoy.

b)   Fishing in protected areas is prohibited, especially lobster and conch; spearfishing is discouraged. Regulations have been proposed to reflect this attitude. It is hoped that parks will help nature replenish surrounding areas.

c)   Litter not! The tiny pop-top of a beer or soft drink can cut a foot or kill a fish. Put your waste into the trash containers you will find in the area.

2   Take care not to damage delicate life.

a)   When anchoring boats, look for bare sand or rock: corals and seagrass are damaged by anchors. Moorings are provided at many anchorages. Please use them!

b)   When snorkelling or diving, keep flippers away from delicate corals. Do not stand on them.

A brief description of the parks and preserves of the British Virgin Islands follows — each has a unique place in these 'treasure islands'.

Tortola

Rain forest   (92 acres) on the Road Town side of Sage Mountain, the highest point on Tortola (1780 feet), it contains some of the last remnants of rain forest which originally grew on the higher islands in the Virgins. Since most of the original forest was used for furniture making and boat building, re-afforestation has been under way for 20 years. Trails are marked, and species are being labelled. From Doty Junction an unsurfaced road leads up to a parking area where a trail leads to the entrance gate.

Botanic gardens   (2.8 acres) are set in the middle of Road Town on Tortola, adjacent to the recreation ground. This garden for the people was established as a place to conserve and display much of the flora of the islands. There is a medicinal or bush garden which includes herbs and plants traditionally used in curing illnesses, a garden called the 'Heliconia' which dis-

Cane Garden Bay on Tortola's north shore   (*Michael Bourne*)

plays a collection of members of the banana family, flora of the sea-shore, cacti and other succulent plants and grasses, and a special Christmas blooming garden. A recent joint project of the B.V.I. Botanic Society, the government, and scores of volunteers, its goal was to foster public awareness of local flora, and of the need to protect the environment.

Queen Elizabeth II Park   (0.7 acres) is a small recreational facility located on the shore below Government House in Road Town.

Windmill ruin   (0.9 acres) is a recently acquired historic site containing one of the few ruins of a windmill preserved from the plantation period when they were used to crush sugar-cane. A right turn off the Brewer's Bay road leads to the ruin on Mount Healthy.

Fat Hog's Bay Pond   (12 acres) is a protected area and bird sanctuary to the west of Fat Hog's Bay on Tortola.

Virgin Gorda

Virgin Gorda Peak   (265 acres) includes the highest point on this island and the 100' contour forms the lower boundary. There is an observation point and trails lead off the road between the Valley and Gun Creek. Within the confines of the above 100' level are the **copper mines** which no longer operate but the ruins are a definite part of island heritage.

Little Fort   (36 acres). Few remains are left of the fort which stood on the point. There is no trail through the difficult boulder terrain and the area serves as a wildlife refuge.

Spring Bay and the Crawl   (5.5 acres). An avenue of palms leads to the beach which is adjacent to Spring Bay. A circle of large boulders forms a natural corral where fish and turtles were kept in earlier times. A turning off the road to the Baths leads to a car park where the trail continues to the beach.

The Baths   (4 acres). This popular tourist attraction is a highlight on Virgin Gorda. Massive granite boulders lying helterskelter make a series of grottoes and caves with a sandy floor where the sea laps in to form attractive pools. The boulders extend under the sea, and the submerged boulders provide scenic snorkelling. They can also be reached by boat (a day anchorage, not good for overnight), or by road from Spanish Town on Virgin Gorda, where a trail leads to the beach from the roundabout at the end of the Baths road.

Devils Bay   (58 acres) lies south of the Baths at the southern tip of Virgin Gorda. There is a very attractive bay enclosed by giant boulders providing a good snorkelling area. A trail to the beach from the roundabout at the end of the road is planned.

Fallen Jerusalem   (30 acres) is an islet immediately south of Virgin Gorda made up of enormous granite boulders. Goats have been removed to protect the vegetation and prevent disturbance to birdlife.

A quiet, unspoiled corner of Tortola   (*G. W. Lennox*)

Other islands

Flamingo Pond (1147 acres) lies on the northern coral island of Anegada. It serves as a sanctuary for water birds which feed and breed in the rich salt pond and mangrove habitat. It is accessible by air and boat.

Wreck of the Rhone (800 acres). This marine park encompasses the remains of the RMS *Rhone* lying in 40–90 feet of water west of Salt Island. The 310 foot steamship sank in a hurricane in 1867. The anchor (140 lb) was lost off Great Harbour on Peter Island, and forms an additional area of the Park, as does the thirty-four-acre Dead Chest Island. The *Rhone* is a very popular dive site, and mooring buoys are provided for yachts at Lee Bay, Salt Island, to protect the wreck and marine life from anchor damage.

Planned protected areas

In addition to the national parks already designated, the National Parks Trust is planning to set up a number of protected areas which have unique features that need protection from the increasing pressures of more and more visitors.

Horseshoe Reef surrounds Anegada stretching for 17 nautical miles. It is estimated that 100 ships have been wrecked since 1600 on the complex of coral reefs here. Thirty species of coral and 185 species of fish have been recorded. Snorkelling and diving are excellent.

North Sound The islets and reefs that encompass the north side of North Sound are a unique barrier that makes this one of the most protected bays in the islands. Beautiful unspoiled reefs teeming with marine life make this whole area a fascinating place for snorkelling and diving.

The Dogs (165.6 acres of land, 4435 acres of sea) are an isolated group of small islands in the channel between Tortola and Virgin Gorda. The reefs and ledges are popular dive sites. Protected here are coral reefs and natural vegetation and sea-bird nesting. West Dog, the most westerly of the group, is already a bird sanctuary.

The Baths   (140 acres of land, 900 acres of sea). This will link up several existing national park areas, and will include the marine habitat of the islets south of Virgin Gorda. The most striking feature on land is the massive boulder formations which extend under the sea.

The Tobagos   (274 acres of land, 710 acres of sea). Great and Little Tobago Islands are the most westerly islands of the B.V.I., lying west of Jost Van Dyke. Here the reefs' natural vegetation and sea bird colonies will be protected.

Norman Island   (10 acres of land, 910 acres of sea). The caves at Treasure Point are reputed to be old hiding places for pirates' treasure, and are popular snorkelling sites, while the bight at Norman Island is a favourite overnight anchorage. Also in-cluded are Pelican Island and The Indians, popular dive sites.

Sandy Cay, Sandy Spit and Green Cay   (30 acres of land, 660 acres of sea). These are small islets off the east coast of Jost Van Dyke, with exceptionally fine coral reefs. They are popular snorkelling spots.

Great Harbour   This deep water bay on Peter Island has long been a fishing ground where beach seines can operate. Boats are prohibited from anchoring or encroaching in areas that may conflict with seine operations.

Note   Please see the map on pages 2/3 for the locations of the national parks and protected areas.

8 History and Government

The pre-Columbian history of the settlement of the Caribbean islands by migratory tribes of Indians is an interesting story, which includes the displacement of the peaceful Arawaks by the more aggressive and warlike Caribs who met the first Europeans. This story is wide-ranging, best told in a history book covering all the Caribbean islands, not in a guide book covering a small island group. So we leave this subject to the students and scholars and confine our historical account to events that specifically affected and were unique to the B.V.I. and its people; and we begin our history with the settlement of these islands by the Europeans.

Although the Dutch were the first European settlers of these islands, permanent settlement did not really begin until the early 1700s, after Britain was able to secure its position of control of the sea lanes in the eastern Caribbean. During this period the British manorial estate and plantation system was introduced, based on the cultivation of sugar and cotton, and the importation of slaves to work the fields.

Although the 1700s were a period of relative prosperity and political stability in the Caribbean, the Virgin Islands — located at the extreme western edge of Britain's eastern Caribbean island holdings — took on many of the aspects of a frontier community. Various accounts tell of a lack of law and order, that the islands were still a refuge for pirates, and that they became a base for illegal trade with both the French and the Spaniards.

In spite of this turmoil, more and more of the island lands

were placed under cultivation, and by the middle of the eighteenth century there were about 1,200 white inhabitants, and about 6,000 non-white. Although this was a generally prosperous period for the planters of the West Indies, and the Virgin Islands shared in this prosperity, these islands were only marginally productive when compared to the larger islands due to the steep terrain and the scant rainfall. While profits and fortunes were made, there were also losses and bankruptcies.

By the end of that century, however, Britain's preoccupation with the Napoleonic wars and unrest and revolts among the slaves of the West Indies caused the islands' economy to fall into a long decline. A disastrous shock to the economy occurred in 1819, when a devastating hurricane roared in, levelling buildings, destroying machinery and killing people and cattle. The damage was staggering.

Emancipation of the slaves came in 1834, but this was replaced by an apprenticeship system — another form of economic bondage of the former slaves — that led to continued unrest. The economic decline continued as political instability and government mismanagement led to a tax revolt in 1853

Government House and Governor's Office, Road Town, Tortola   (*Michael Bourne*)

that swept the British Virgin Islands, resulting in the departure of all the white inhabitants, and the destruction of the plantation estate system. With the departure of the white planters, the former slaves either bought or took over the land, resulting in the ownership of the land by the island residents who remained.

For the next forty years, the islands were in a state of both economic and political stagnation. Britain provided only token government, as the islands were placed in the Federation of Leeward Islands, and received only occasional visits from the officials of the Crown. Many of the inhabitants left, seeking employment in the neighbouring islands. From a high point of about 10,000 people at the beginning of the nineteenth century, the population declined to about 5,000 at the beginning of the twentieth century.

At the turn of the century, two modest but important steps were taken to restore the ties between the people of the islands and Great Britain. First, a Governor-in-Council was established with a full-time representative of the government in residence on the islands, and second, compulsory education in schools patterned after the British school system was introduced. In addition, a move to revive the islands' economy was made when the government set up an agricultural experimental station.

Progress was still slow, and for another fifty years the economy relied on the meagre agricultural resources of the islands, supplemented by financial support from Britain. Despite the handicaps of difficult terrain and uncertain water supply, agriculture and stock farming on small owner-occupied holdings raised crops for domestic use and export primarily to the U.S. Virgin Islands. Fishing also supplied food for the table, and some excess for sale to their neighbours. To supplement their income, many inhabitants took jobs in St Thomas, which came under U.S. control in 1917, and many of them stayed there to become permanent residents.

During the 1940s, while the U.S. Government under Franklin D. Roosevelt was pouring money into the U.S. Virgins creating jobs and prosperity, the British government was doing so little that one historian said that their colonial policy was the equivalent of no policy. The British Virgin Islands became Britain's forgotten colony. The story is told that when Winston Churchill was asked if he knew where the British Virgin Islands were, he replied that he had no idea, but was quite certain they were a great distance from the Isle of Man.

The end of World War II saw the beginning of the resurgence of the British Virgin Islands, both economically and politically. The war and post-war economic boom in the U.S. Virgin Islands had a strong impact on the neighbouring British group — not only by providing more jobs for migrating Tortolians, but also by attracting tourists, who were quick to see not only the natural beauty of all the islands, but to recognise and savour the quiet ambience of the British islands, when compared to the frenetic hustle-bustle of St Thomas.

During this period there were continuing close ties between the peoples of the two Virgin Island groups. Several suggestions were made that the U.S. should take over the British islands, and some officials even recommended a plebiscite on the subject in the British islands in which they felt certain the people

Colourful old houses, now used as shops and offices, line Road Town's Main Square   (*Michael Bourne*)

would support such a change. Fortunately for the British Virgin Islands and their people, clearer thinking prevailed, and the islands did not succumb to progress — American style.

The post-war era also brought demands by the people for a more representative government, which signalled the demise of the old colonial system and the breakup of Britain's Leeward Islands colony. First, the British Virgin Islands withdrew from the Federation of the Leeward Islands and became a political entity. Then by a series of moves they were granted more and more autonomy and self-government, combined with greater grants-in-aid to help build up the islands' economy. During the 1960s the British Colonial Office took additional steps resulting in a study being made to determine the future of the colony. The study recommended, among other things, that the colony remain British, and that steps be taken to encourage tourism as the future economic base for the islands.

This culminated in 1967 with the adoption of a new constitution under which broad powers were given to the islanders to participate in the government of their islands. Except for a few minor amendments, this constitutional form of government

A rooster crosses Main Street, Road Town in perfect safety (*Michael Bourne*)

is still in effect. Practically, the British Virgin Islands are today a self-governed Territory of the United Kingdom, under an elected Legislative and Executive Council who select a Chief Minister, with final approval of legislative acts resting in a Governor appointed by the Crown. It is a system that has worked well, attested by the fact of continuing political and economic stability.

Historical milestones

1493 The Virgin Islands discovered and named by Columbus.
1555 Spanish forces invaded the islands, defeating and annihilating the West Indians.
1585 Sir Francis Drake passed through en route to Puerto Rico.
1595 Sir Francis Drake anchored in Virgin Gorda Sound.
1648 Temporary settlement of Tortola by Dutch buccaneers.
1672 Islands captured from the Dutch and annexed to England's other Caribbean islands.
1717 First census — showed 795 white, 547 non-white.
     First Quaker missionaries arrived.
1752 The Virgin Islands were the principal suppliers of cotton from the West Indies to Britain.
1773 The first constitutional government established.
1787 The first post office was opened in Road Town.
1803 Road Town was proclaimed a free port.
1805 Census showed 1,300 white, 9,220 non-white.
1807 Britain abolished the slave trade in all her colonies.
1834 Britain abolished slavery. Over 5,000 slaves were freed.
1853 A tax revolt by former slaves drove the white planters from the island, ending the plantation estate system.
1872 Federation of the Leeward Islands formed, including the British Virgin Islands.
1890 Compulsory education was introduced.
1900 An agricultural experimental station was opened as a result of a prior visit by a Royal Commission.
1901 Census showed 2 white, 4,906 non-white.
1902 Legislative Council abolished. The government of the

Leeward Islands became the sole legislature.

1940 United States military installations constructed on St Thomas. Many British Virgin Islanders employed.

1943 Secondary education was introduced.

1946 Census showed 40 white, 6,468 non-white.

1950 The Legislative Council was reconstituted.

1956 The Federation of the Leeward Islands dissolved. A Commissioner of the Virgin Islands appointed as Administrator.

1964 The first resort hotel, developed by Laurence Rockefeller, opened at Little Dix Bay on Virgin Gorda.

1966 Her Majesty Queen Elizabeth II and His Royal Highness The Duke of Edinburgh visited the islands.

1967 A new constitution was adopted granting greater self-government under a ministerial system.
The islands became a Territory of the United Kingdom.
United States currency became the sole legal tender.

1969 Development of Wickham's Cay in Road Harbour began. Population estimated at 9,700.

1980 Continued strong economic growth supported by tourism.
Census showed population of 10,985.

9 The People — in Legend, in History, and Today

The Pirates

That there were pirates in the British Virgin Islands in its earliest days is undoubtedly fact. But since there were no historians in the islands then to record their activities, most of what we know about them comes down as legend and lore. Here are some of the tales of pirates that are told in the islands.

Just east of Deadman's Bay on Peter Island is the islet of Dead Chest. This is a shortened version of its original name of Dead Man's Chest, and this is the tale of how it got its name.

The pirate Blackbeard was anchored in Deadman's Bay after completing one of his forays, where his men were dividing up the spoils. An argument occurred about the division, and it led to mutiny by some of the crew, finally settled by marooning fifteen mutineers with some rum and their sea chests on the islet off the bay. Blackbeard then left with the rest of his men, to return there much later. Upon his return, they rowed over to the islet in their long-boat to find only the skeletons of the marooned men and their sea chests. Hence the pirate shanty:

> Fifteen men on a dead man's chest,
> Yo Ho Ho and a bottle of rum.
> Drink and the devil have done the rest,
> Yo Ho Ho and a bottle of rum.

High on a hill on the north coast of Tortola, just south of Cane Garden Bay, is the ruin of an old church, which was St Michael's Church, the church of the pirate priest, Audain. There are two versions of this tale. One version says that most of his parishioners were fellow-pirates, and the church became a look-out for ships passing in the waters between Tortola and Jost Van Dyke. When a ship was sighted, church service was abruptly terminated, and the pirate priest and his parishioners boarded their own vessel anchored in Cane Garden Bay to give chase.

Another version says that he only watched for other known pirate vessels, and preyed only on them, allowing innocent vessels to pass through. Whichever version is true, the legend of the pirate priest is strong in the islands, and an abandoned cannon and wheel found near some masonry at Canon Point north of Cane Garden Bay indicates the possibility of an old fortress or strong point there long ago.

Beef Island, just east of Tortola, was so named because for generations it was used only as a place to run cattle and, as late as 1935, the only inhabitants were those so engaged. This is fact. The legend says that a Mrs O'Brien (or was it O'Grady?) the owner of the cattle on Beef Island when the islands were just beginning to be settled, sold beef to anyone, including the few pirates who were still passing through. The pirates, having

An aerial view of the British Virgin Islands, showing Maya Cove, one of the many safe anchorages once used by pirates   (G. W. Lennox)

'taking' ways, started poaching her cattle, and she felt the need to stop them. So she sent out a message, inviting them all to a beef barbecue on the island; during the barbecue she served her pirate guests tea laced with arsenic. She was never again bothered.

The Bight of Norman Island, today one of the favourite anchorages of charter boats and visiting yachtsmen because of its shelter and seclusion, was also a favourite anchorage of the pirates for the same reason. The story is told of how they would hide their vessels in The Bight, post look-outs on the high surrounding hills and, when an unsuspecting vessel came too close, sail out to intercept and maraud.

There are also several tales of treasure being buried on this island, including the treasure of the pirate Norman, for whom the island is named. Another treasure tale is contained in a letter telling of a conspiracy involving the mystery of the treasure of the *Nuestra Senora*, sunk off the Carolina coast and never found. Believed stolen by the Governor of Santo Domingo, it may have been placed on another boat that was intercepted by pirates, and ultimately buried on Norman Island.

There is also a tale of treasure found in one of the water-level caves near Treasure Point, and some steps carved out of the rock in the cave are pointed out as leading to a ledge where the treasure was hidden. True or not, these tales have brought treasure hunters to this island from time to time, still digging in hope but, as far as is known, in vain.

Perhaps any treasure here is protected by a superstition common to all the Caribbean islands. This says that treasure was buried in earthenware jars by the Spaniards, whose ghosts surround the jars to protect them from discovery and theft. Should anyone find out where the jars are hidden — and this could only happen in a dream — the finders would have to face the ghostly wrath of the ancient caretakers before they could claim the treasure.

The early Quakers

During the middle of the seventeenth century, England was

swept by religious dissension, and one of the most 'radical' of these dissenting groups was the Society of Friends, whose members are commonly called Quakers. Persecuted in England, many of them, like other dissenting groups, fled to the New World. The history of the migration of the Quakers under William Penn to Pennsylvania is well known.

Not so well known is that many Quakers also migrated to the West Indies. The first Quakers arrived in Barbados in 1655. They gradually spread to the other islands, possibly arriving in the Virgin Islands in the early 1700s, where they founded colonies on both Virgin Gorda and Tortola in 1727. Out of this Quaker heritage two men rose in the islands to make their marks in history: Dr John Lettsom and his close friend William Thornton.

John Lettsom was born in 1744 on the island of Little Jost Van Dyke, the son of an English planter who had estates both on that island and across the channel at Cane Garden Bay on Tortola. At an early age he was sent back to England for schooling, not to return until 1767 after the death of his father. He remained in the islands only long enough to help settle his father's estate, free the slaves he had inherited, and practise medicine there long enough to establish a nest-egg to pay for his return to England, even though he had not yet completed

Local transport old and new   (*B.V.I. Tourist Board*)

his medical course and received his MD. It only took him six months to earn about £2,000; half of that he gave his mother, the other half took him back to England.

He finished his training, got his MD degree, and pursued a distinguished medical career in England. A wealthy man and philanthropist, he gave to many organisations, and was identified with two both as a donor and founder — the London Medical Society and the Royal Humane Society. He was also a prolific correspondent and writer, and wrote many times to his fellow Quaker and islander, William Thornton, who resided in the U.S.A. Most of his writing was done in his carriage while he was making his medical rounds. Whether it was written about him or by him is not certain, but he is remembered by many for this piece of doggerel:

> I, John Lettsom
> Blisters, bleeds and sweats 'em.
> If, after that, they please to die
> I, John Lettsom.

The other famous island Quaker, William Thornton, was born on Jost Van Dyke in 1759. He, too, left the islands at an early age to complete his schooling in England. Like John Lettsom, he made medicine his career, and received his MD in 1784. He returned to Tortola soon after graduation, but then went to Philadelphia, and became a United States citizen. He also became a self-taught architect there. In 1790 he returned to Tortola to practise medicine while he settled an inheritance. Like Lettsom, he, too, had inherited slaves; but his interest went beyond just freeing his own slaves, and he became active in one of the movements to send freed slaves back to Africa.

While in Tortola, he heard of the competition to design the new Capitol in Washington, D.C. and even though his designs were received months after the competition was closed, they were accepted. He returned to Washington to become one of the city commissioners. He was a talented man, for in addition to being a physician and self-taught architect he was also an inventor — and participated with John Fitch in the development of the paddlewheel steamboat. He served as the first superintendent of the U.S. patent office from 1802 until his death in 1828. The ruins of the Thornton greathouse are located on Tortola near Sea Cow's Bay, not far from the road to West End.

One of the Quaker settlements was at Fat Hog's Bay. Samuel and Mary Nottingham, the Quaker owners of estate Long Look on that bay, not only freed their slaves in 1778, but gave to the freed slaves and their descendants communal title to the property. This generous act created cloudy titles to these lands for almost 200 years, finally settled by the present government.

A poignant story is told of how Long Look got its name. When the slaves arrived, they were taken off the vessels bringing them from Africa at Soper's Hole at the west end of Tortola, then were marched on foot to the plantations where they were to be settled. When this group finally climbed over the last of the many hills from Soper's Hole and came down into the valley surrounding Fat Hog's Bay, a vista opened up between the islands across the waters to the south-east. This was the 'long look' back to their African homeland.

The Quaker movement gradually died out, and the monthly meeting was abandoned in 1762. Though a few Quakers remained on, this was effectively the end of the movement in Tortola. Today, all that remains are the memories and a crumbling cemetery near Fat Hog's Bay.

King Sugar and the planters

The story of Britain's participation in the slave trade, the rise and growth of the plantation system on the British colonies of the West Indies, and the profits of the planters in the production of both cotton and sugar based on slave labour, has been told many times and need not be repeated here. What is of interest are some of the special circumstances that existed in this small group of islands, physically separated from Britain's other Caribbean islands, and at the western edge of her Leeward Islands Caribbean empire. It created a way of life that was in some aspects quite different from the larger islands.

The reins of government were much looser here, resulting in

many reports that the islands were in an almost continuous state of anarchy. Several accounts mention continuing piracy in the islands, and that the islands were in a state of disorder and neglect, offering a base for illegal trade with the Spaniards, the French and the Dutch during this period.

As in the early frontier communities of the U.S.A., the gun apparently replaced the law, with piracy and smuggling substituting for the North American counterparts of cattle rustling and horse stealing. This lasted until the middle of the eighteenth century, and the coming of a more settled group of small planters. Even then George Suckling, the first Chief Justice of the Virgin Islands, found in 1778 that the white inhabitants were 'hospitable, well meaning, honest people', but that religion and morals were at a low ebb and a riotous and lawless minority defied all authority, so that Tortola 'presented a shocking scene of anarchy'.

By the last quarter of the eighteenth century, sugar and slavery were the foundations upon which rested almost the whole economic life of all the Leeward Islands and, from what we read, conditions here were not much different from the other British holdings. The Virgin Islands slave act of 1783 was cited as one of the most oppressive in all of the islands, regulating the lives of the slaves so rigidly that even their funerals were controlled.

The aftermath

Under conditions like these, it is no wonder there were periodic revolts, even after slavery was abolished. In the final revolt, triggered by a repressive tax, the island people were called to united action by the blowing of horns made from conch shells. The revolt succeeded, and created a situation unique in these islands. All the white minority left, the freed slaves completely took over the islands, and a new era began.

The price of real freedom was neglect, but the people wanted it that way. They had had enough, and literally went back to the bush. Contact with the few British officials who occasionally called was avoided. There are no written accounts of this

period, but the few surviving oral records tell a story of poverty
and hardship, of many giving up and leaving. Those families
that stuck it out drew closer.

The abandoned land was simply taken over and made into
smallholdings where the people managed to survive by farming
and fishing, and with money sent back by family members who
had secured jobs on other islands. It was a long, slow road back,
and many years before there was mutual trust between the
people of the islands and the representatives of government.

The recent years

It was the resurgence of the U.S. Virgin Islands that set in
motion the forces that began the re-vitalisation of the British
Islands, and the beginnings of a partnership between the people
and the government. In the early years of this period, the
B.V.I. were considered by many a 'poor relative' of the U.S.
group, and it was during this period that the ties between the
two island groups became more binding. So many of the families on the B.V.I. had relatives in St Thomas that it was
estimated that in the 1970s over half of that island's residents

Girl Guides on parade   (*B.V.I. Tourist Board*)

either came from Tortola or were descendants of Tortolans.

Tourism became the keystone of prosperity in the U.S. Virgin Islands, and it spilled over into the B.V.I. By now, the people of the B.V.I. had a greater voice in their government, and a firm policy was developed to improve their economy, with tourism as the base. The development plan here, though, was to be more controlled, to eliminate some of the mistakes seen on the neighbouring islands.

Part of this policy was designed around a greater participation by the island residents in the coming prosperity. The people demanded this, reflecting their independence of attitude, and a capitalistic approach to their future — a result of their past isolation, and because most of them were already small land-owners. The people are remarkably close-knit, a heritage from the days of want and neglect, and of inter-marriage among the surviving families that remained on the islands. One historian, writing of the people of the British Virgin Islands has said, 'Common experiences under difficult economic circumstances ... contributed toward the creation of an indissoluble bond between all sectors of the population which is still a characteristic of society.'[1]

The small size of the society on these British islands supports a familiarity among them all that makes it hard to sustain hostility. People who have to live on the same small islands all their lives quickly learn how to get along with those whose opinions may differ. Three characteristics of this small indigenous population seem to stand out — reserve, dignity, and pride. The visitor here will never be asked for a hand-out.

The typical islander is essentially conservative, both in demeanour and dress. Street dress here is casual, but short shorts, bare midriffs, swim-suits and bikinis are simply not accepted as appropriate dress on the streets. Visitors are asked to confine these to the beaches and pools.

Although most of the resident islanders are British citizens, there is a special privileged class of citizens on these islands,

---

[1] I. Dookhan, *A History of the British Virgin Islands: Some Notes on its Writing and Bibliography*, 1967, p. 6.

found nowhere else to our knowledge, called the 'Belonger' — one who was born and raised in the islands, or is related by marriage to one who is island-born. The 'Belonger' receives special rights and consideration from the government, especially in employment.

Island food and drink

> Fungi, Gundy, Callaloo.
> Plantains, Seagrapes, boiled Foo-Foo.
> Paw Paw, Soursop, thick Goat Stew,
> Johnny Cakes and Jug Jug too!

This short rhyme portrays the most popular fruits, vegetables and island dishes found throughout the Caribbean. Interestingly, the names accurately come from the islanders' past but, in plain English, today it would read as fried cornmeal with okr , boiled fish with hot peppers, spinach soup, cooking bananas, boiled and pounded yam, cassava, or mashed plantain and curried goat stew.

British Virgin Island food is a pot-pourri representing the food culture of the various peoples who have inhabited the Caribbean islands over the centuries, coupled with tropical fare developed from produce grown locally, and the fruits of the seas surrounding the islands, with a touch of British cooking techniques added.

Island hotels feature spectacular buffets. A speciality is glazed whole poached fish with fresh oysters and salmon mousse in mushroom caps   (*Larry and Reba Shepard*)

Hotels tend to take the path of least resistance and use mostly imported foods, but the better chefs make an effort to combine both the best imports and locally grown and caught items. If you find a hotel that serves local food regularly, you will have found one of the hotels that have a better cuisine.

A centuries-old tradition in the islands is dining under the stars, with outdoor cookouts. For special occasions, whole pigs are not infrequently roasted. Other times, ribs and chicken are cooked over local charcoal on an open grill. Side dishes will often include a dish of **Fungi**, a cornmeal starch dish which is served in lieu of less readily available potatoes. Here are some island recipes which have been handed down in the B.V.I. and are still in use today.

FUNGI

To 5 cups rapidly boiling water
Add   Salt to taste
Sprinkle on slowly   2 cups cornmeal

Allow water to boil over meal a few minutes, stirring briskly to prevent lumping. When well combined,

Add   2 tablespoons shortening.

Cover and steam for 5–10 minutes, stirring often. Serve hot.

Variations
Fungi with okra Add okra cut in small pieces to water and allow to boil a few minutes before adding meal.
Sweet fungi Instead of okras, add $\frac{1}{2}$ cup raisins and $\frac{1}{2}$ cup sugar to water and allow to boil a few minutes first.
Savoury fungi Add your choice of spices combinations to water before adding cornmeal.

Another locally grown food, much in use as a vegetable, is dasheen or eddoe leaves, used in making dishes called **Callaloo**. Callaloo is also an alternative name for spinach.

CALLALOO AND RICE

Cut into small pieces   225 g ($\frac{1}{2}$ pound) salt meat

In a large pan,
Simmer about 10 minutes in 1 cup water
Wash and cut up   675 g (1½ pounds) callaloo leaves
                            12 okras
                            1 clove garlic
                            2 small tomatoes
                            1 onion

Add these to the meat. Cover saucepan tightly and simmer 5 minutes.

Add   1 tablespoon lime juice
Sprinkle in   2 cups rice
Cook until rice grains are soft. Serve hot.

Callaloo soup   is similar, but without the rice, and often with crab added.

The cooking banana, or plantain, is also a starch, and not a sweet eating fruit. It must be cooked, and the easiest method is called:

FOO FOO
(Pounded plantains)

Boil   3 green, 1 ripe but firm plantains

When soft pound them in a large mortar.
Dip pestle in cold water between pounding to prevent sticking.

When smooth, mix with   2 tablespoons butter
                            Salt to taste
Keep warm.

When visiting the British Virgin Islands, one food item which should not be overlooked is the pumpkin soup. While most people think of pumpkin as a pie ingredient, the local residents use it as a vegetable. There are endless ways to make this soup, but this is one favourite:

PUMPKIN SOUP

Slice and lightly fry	2 onions
In	2 tablespoons butter
Add peeled and cut up	450 g (1 lb) pumpkin
	$\frac{1}{2}$ c split peas (soaked 4 hrs)
	black pepper to taste
	2 cabbage leaves, chopped finely
	piece fresh thyme or 1 teaspoon dry
	225 g ($\frac{1}{2}$ lb) salt meat

Cover with water and simmer about 1 hour.

Locally available and plentiful, coconuts are used in a variety of ways, and they add valuable nutrition to anything they are used in. One favourite:

COCONUT BUNS

Sift together	4 cups, flour
	2 teaspoons baking powder
	$\frac{1}{2}$ teaspoon salt
Add	150 g (6 oz) sugar
Add	1 egg, lightly beaten with $\frac{3}{4}$ cup
	milk or coconut water
	100 g ($\frac{1}{4}$ lb) shortening
	1 teaspoon vanilla essence
Stir in	2 cups grated coconut
Flour, then stir in	150 g (6 oz) raisins

Blend ingredients well.
Knead dough slightly on floured board.
Shape into large buns and put into greased loaf pan, filling only $\frac{2}{3}$ of each pan.
Dust with fine sugar. Bake in moderate oven.
Makes 2 loaves or about 12 buns.

POACHED FISH

For an elegant poached fillet of white fish, simply combine B.V.I. seasoning salt with lime or lemon juice. Marinate fish for 30 minutes. Add white wine to cover, and bake until fish flakes with a fork when tested. Serve hot with sauce and boiled white rice.

WEST INDIAN FISH SAUCE

If you want your fish to be a bit more elaborate, another sauce can be made by boiling 1 sliced onion and 1 sliced green and 1 sliced red sweet pepper in enough water to cover. When vegetables are tender, strain, reserving liquid. Mix 1 tablespoon flour with $\frac{1}{2}$ cup good dry white wine, and add to hot liquid. Heat to thicken, add salt and pepper to taste, return vegetables to pan, and serve over poached fish. (Fish may be poached in liquid while cooking vegetables if you wish.)

A report on island cooking would be incomplete without a recipe for their hot sauce. There are different sauces, all hot, and available in island markets. Locally grown peppers are tiny, but fierce. Care must be taken in handling, especially in cutting, to be sure that nothing that has touched a pepper touches an eye.

PICKLED HOT PEPPERS

Cut into pieces and remove	
seeds from	225 g ($\frac{1}{2}$ lb) hot peppers
or leave whole, as you prefer.	
In a saucepan, combine	2 cups white vinegar
	1 tablespoon salt
	50 g (2 oz) sugar
	2 tablespoons chopped onion
Add	peppers

Bring to a boil and simmer for 5 minutes.
Cool.

Add	few ($\frac{1}{2}$ teaspoon) peppercorns
and	$\frac{1}{4}$ cup rum

Pour into sterilised containers and allow to steep for a few days before using.

No food and drink list of the islands would be complete without their recipe for:

ISLAND RUM PUNCH

Basically, the punch is made up of:
One Sour
Two Sweet
Three Strong
Four Weak.
In the islands, 'Sour' is fresh lime juice.
'Sweet' can be honey, syrup, white sugar, brown sugar.
'Strong' is island rum which is at least 90% proof.
'Weak' is juices, preferably fresh. Guava juice is excellent, but cut down on the 'sweet' if using all guava juice. An acceptable substitute is canned fruit juice. A good combination is $\frac{1}{3}$ grapefruit juice, $\frac{1}{3}$ orange juice and $\frac{1}{3}$ pineapple juice.
Mix well, serve over ice, but watch out — its delicious taste can lead to over-indulgence.[2]

Religion

Islanders have a strong spiritual and religious background, that also goes back to the very early days. Christian missionaries arrived on most Caribbean islands only shortly after the arrival of the first slaves. In the early days, the religious spirit was expressed in both Christian rites, and in superstition and magic carried over from the ex-slaves' West African heritage. Early Christian holidays became intertwined with African customs, and Christmas especially became a time of religious fervour and celebration.

Today the religious spirit is still strong, as evidenced by the numerous churches on the islands. A large number of Protestant denominations are represented here today, from Anglican to Pentacostal, as well as Catholic. The attendance and

[2] Shepard, Reba E, *The Charter Cookbook.* Macmillan, London and Basingstoke 1985.

support given by the people to their churches is probably better than that given in many so-called 'developed' countries.

Festival

Virtually all of the Caribbean islands have an annual Carnival, celebrated on each island at different times, and each in its own way. While no two are exactly alike, in every case it is the biggest and most important party of the year. The B.V.I. Festival is a three-day bash during the first week of August.

Originally a religious rite, later a celebration of freedom from bondage, today it is an opportunity to cast off the cares and conventions of daily life, let down the hair, and celebrate.

The first evidence of festival time in the B.V.I. is when the booths start going up on Wickham's Cay, and the carnival rides start assembling. Quickly it becomes a time of eating, drinking and dancing to the rhythm of calypso music. This is when the island chefs turn out their best johnny-cakes, callaloo, foo foo, served up with maubi, island rum, or maybe even some hoarded guavaberry wine.

Practically, island businesses close for the three days of festi-

A Carnival Queen   (*Caribbean Images Ltd*)

val, and many absent relatives return to the islands to be with family and friends. This is a time when the best traits of the islanders surface — when they rally with pride around the music, food, dance and spirit that is their heritage.

Sports in the islands

One of the most active organisers and sponsors of sporting events for the residents of the islands is the B.V.I. Yacht Club, located in Road Town, near Fort Burt Marina. Their activities are three-fold — involving tournaments and competitions in rugby, fishing and sailing.

Rugby A number of local events and tournaments are sponsored throughout the year, which is topped off by the big event of the year, the International Rugby Festival usually held in September. This event involves a weekend of seven-a-side rugby competition, and numerous social events for players, supporters and spectators.

Fishing Both inshore and offshore fishing tournaments are held throughout the year with junior and senior classes, and prizes are given both on the basis of the number of fish caught and the weight. The principal annual event is the international billfish tournament, usually held during the full moon in August, with major prizes awarded for catches of blue marlin, and minor prizes for the heaviest wahoo, tuna, and kingfish.

Sailing The B.V.I. Yacht Club has a very active sailing programme, hosting a sailing event every month of the year. Local races include their January Polar bear race, February's St Valentine's day race and Hood pursuit race, March Winds race, Maypole race, TeUnaine race, Virgin's cup, August Anegada race, September's Equinox race, October's St Ursula's day race, November's Pusser's Rum round-Tortola race, and December's Christmas Commodore's race.

The big international event of the year is the annual B.V.I. Spring Regatta, held in April as the second leg of the Caribbean Ocean Racing Triangle (C.O.R.T.). This event draws sailing yachts and spectators from not only Caribbean Islands but also the U.S.A. It follows the Copa Velasco in Puerto Rico, and precedes the international Rolex cup Regatta in St Thomas.

Organised by the B.V.I. Yacht Club in conjunction with the B.V.I. Hotel and Commerce Association, The B.V.I. Spring Regatta is the sailing and social event of the season.

Conclusion

Today, the B.V.I. reports one of the highest standards of living in the West Indies, only slightly lower than their American neighbours. Yet they have retained their uniqueness, and a society that many believe offers a superior quality of life to that in the neighbouring islands. The pace is slower, the people are fewer, more law-abiding — and more friendly. Everything is on a smaller, quieter scale.

Like the British Isles, these are 'tight little isles', and the atmosphere here is British, rather than American. One of the slogans in promotions used by the B.V.I. Tourist Board, is 'Yes, We're Different'. And indeed they are. Although 'different' does not necessarily mean 'better', there are many who believe that this difference really is better.

Baseball is one of the many sports popular in the Islands   (*B.V.I. Tourist Board*)

10 The Economy Today — Commerce and Industry

Agriculture

For islands whose economy was originally built on farming, island agriculture today does not show it. Once almost all food necessities were raised here, and even some food exported. Today, less than one-third of the local food requirement is locally grown. Even though the island terrain is unfriendly to farming, more farming has been done in the past than is done now. The vegetables available in the Saturday morning green market are welcome but seasonal and frequently expensive. Local limes, bananas, papayas, coconuts, a few herbs, a few varieties of tomatoes and occasionally local fish and beef, yams and tannia are about all that is available.

A government farming project is still in the pipeline, and free land was made available for gardens and livestock, but little use has been made of it. Most of the food required on the islands is imported. Even the sugar-cane, which was so important in the early history of the islands, is imported for the local rum distillers, except for a small plot grown for show at a local distillery. With most of the food imported from Puerto Rico and the U.S.A., visitors will find food costs high.

Fishing

Commercial fishing has been done by islanders since the early days. Many took to their boats to catch what nature had to offer as a means of survival, selling their catches in the adjoining islands. In the mid-1900s, a toxin found in some species of fish seriously hurt the local industry. Only recently has research in this field made some progress in isolating the types of fish affected, and restored some confidence in locally caught fish. Now, local restaurants proudly proclaim, once again, 'only fresh, local fish served here'. It is important that visitors should be aware that it is illegal for non-B.V. Islanders to remove any marine organism without a recreational fishing permit.

Commercial fishing is still done, principally on Anegada, and the government recently initiated a fishing cooperative in an attempt to restore the industry, but it is still too early to evaluate the results. At present, locally caught fish is available in local markets, but little has been available for export.

Rum distilling and bottling

This is a major industry in adjoining St Croix and Puerto Rico, and is a small, but growing industry in the B.V.I. There are two rum processors — one old, one relatively new. The Callwood Distillery near Cane Garden Bay has been making rum for 200

The Pusser's Rum Company Store and Pub on Front Street
(*Michael Bourne*)

years, using an old copper still that must be seen to be believed. Both light and dark rum are produced and sold in limited quantities.

A more recent entry into this field is Pusser's Rum, which produces a dark rum patterned on and named after the rum famous in the British Navy. The name is used under an agreement in which part of the proceeds of each sale go to a British Navy benevolent fund. Although most of this rum is produced off the islands, it is brought here for bottling and distribution. This enterprise has grown, and now has substantial sales in both the U.S.A. and Canada. The company operates a large retail store in Road Town, with many old Royal Navy artefacts on display, and soon a mail-order catalogue will be introduced.

Cottage industries

In keeping with its policy of creating jobs for local residents, the B.V.I. government encourages so-called cottage industries, occupations where people can work from their homes to create an income for themselves. Some people have artistic ability, and use it in the making of saleable items such as hand-crafted jewellery, hand-woven baskets, watercolour pictures, wood carvings, and collector's items made from shells or coral.

Sometimes these home industries develop into fully-fledged businesses, like the jewellery shop that creates gold and silver designs, or the fabric printing business where cotton is silk-screened with patterns gleaned from local nature, or statues moulded from crushed coral. Others have culinary skills, and either whip up their own recipes of mango or pumpkin chutney, or make West Indian hot sauce, which they bottle and sell. Others pick leaves from various trees and blend them into 'herb-teas' which are sold through the local spice factory. These are packaged in hand-woven baskets, or in silk-screened, hand-made bags, or in jars with brightly coloured, hand-made covers.

Seasoned sea salt

The basic ingredient comes from Salt Island, and is then combined with other herbs and spices such as nutmeg, celery, mace, cloves, garlic, parsley and peppercorn to create a product called 'British Virgin Islands Caribbean Seasoning'. Made and packaged in the B.V.I. it is widely sold in the islands in tourist and gift shops, and is also now being exported.

Private clinic

Road Town is the home of a small private clinic and plastic surgery centre called the Bougainvillaea Clinic. British surgeon Dr Robert Tattersall and his American Associate Dr Ralph Blocksma, aided by a staff of fifteen, have developed a way to combine plastic surgery with a Caribbean holiday for off-island patients. In addition to plastic surgery their practice includes reconstructive, general and gynaecological surgery in an unequalled atmosphere for recuperation.

Newspapers

Two local newspapers are distributed in the islands, whose contents contain mostly items of local interest: *The Island Sun*,

The offices of the *Island Sun* newspaper   (*Michael Bourne*)

published bi-weekly, and the *BVI Beacon*, published weekly. In addition, *The Daily News*, a daily newspaper published in the U.S.V.I. and *USA Today*, also a daily, can be found at many island outlets. Two marine-oriented monthly newspapers are also widely distributed: *Marine Scene*, a monthly supplement of *The Daily News*, and *Caribbean Boating*.

Financial services

Although not as well known as The Bahamas and the Cayman Islands, the British Virgin Islands is a 'tax haven' country, and financial services constitute an important segment of business. There are four major full-service international banks serving the islands in Road Town: one British (Barclays Bank), one Canadian (Bank of Nova Scotia), and two American (Chase Manhattan Bank and First Pennsylvania Bank). There is also a full-service agency of American Express Company.

In addition to the major banks, there are a number of Trust Companies which offer financial consulting services and company formation and management services, some holding general banking licenses and connections with merchant banking services.

Major credit cards and traveller's cheques are honoured by most tourist-oriented establishments, but don't try to cash a personal cheque on an off-island bank account. It takes over three weeks for such cheques to clear, and they are therefore accepted only for delayed deposit.

Tourism

There is no doubt that tourism is the main industry in the B.V.I. Although the government is the second largest employer in the islands, the tourist industry and its satellite businesses is by far the largest, accounting for the bulk of the islands' income, and supporting a relatively high standard of living.

The first luxury resort hotel was opened in 1964 on Virgin Gorda and the first yacht charter operation opened in 1970. These industries have grown until today there are many hotels, a number of which can be classed as de luxe resort hotels, along with additional cottage complexes, guest houses, and holiday homes and villas to accommodate the vacationer.

It is estimated there are now more than 300 charter boats based in the B.V.I., and in addition, almost all of the St Thomas based charter yachts spend the majority of their time in B.V.I. waters, making both Sir Francis Drake Channel and Virgin Gorda Sound, with their surrounding bays and anchorages, alive with bareboat and crewed charter yachts. It has been said that there are more beds on the waters of the B.V.I. than in the hotels.

Resort hotels

Although the growth of tourism is dramatic, it has also been gradual and controlled, slowly and with care to preserve and maintain the unequalled and so-far undisturbed beauty that makes these islands so attractive. Do not expect to find any high-rise Hiltons here. With a single exception, all of the hotels have less than 100 rooms, and that exception has only 131. In every case, the trees and gardens surrounding the buildings are a dominant feature, and the buildings are no higher than the trees that surround them.

In islands girdled by the sea, it should be no surprise that most of the hotels and other land-based tourist accommodation border the sea, so guests may take full advantage of water-oriented activities; whether passive — lying under a beach umbrella on the sand; or active — enjoying such sports as swimming, windsurfing, or snorkelling. Warm and translucent waters, laced with coral reefs, make snorkelling and scuba-diving a memorable experience for most visitors. Some of the hotels are adjuncts of yacht chartering operations, providing a land base for guests for a day or two at either end of their charter trip. Some hotels have teamed up with yacht charter companies to offer a combination package of several days in the hotel and several days on the water.

Most of the resort hotels operate under the American Plan, with meals provided and included in the daily rate. Great pride is taken in the quality of both the food and service provided for guests. Expect to dine well here!

Many of the hotels have special nights for local entertainment, music and dancing to local 'fungi' bands. Some also feature live music every night, in the form of a piano or guitar player. There are no casinos here, and only a few discotheques — 'night life' is not a big thing, but with all the daytime activities most people don't seem to miss it.

Some of the larger hotels offer such other activities as tennis and horseback riding, provide windsurfers or sailing dinghies, and can arrange for their guests to take day sails, go scuba-diving or take a glass bottom boat or snorkelling tour.

Yacht chartering

Sailboat chartering is a major segment of the tourist industry in these islands. Recent government statistics show that over two-thirds of the money spent by tourists here comes from that source — making it an important contributor to the islands' economy. The Sir Francis Drake Channel is literally encircled by islands, giving smooth, protected seas, and Virgin Gorda

Yachts manoeuvre for position during a regatta   (G. W. *Lennox*)

Sound is an immense bay also protected by islands and coral reefs.

When you take smooth seas with light tides and currents, add constant tropical trade winds, season with warm, clear waters, and serve with sheltered anchorages, you have a recipe that has deservedly made the British Virgin Islands the charter sailing capital of the Caribbean, if not the world.

Eleven bareboat charter yacht companies are based here, ten on Tortola, one on Virgin Gorda. They offer a wide selection of sailing yachts, from 30 feet to 60 feet, mostly 'bareboat' — where the guests become their own captain and crew and either do their own provisioning, or purchase a package from their charter company. Some bareboat companies also offer crewed yachts, where a captain, and if desired a cook, are provided. These charters are primarily for a term of a week or more, booked and reserved in advance from the company offices in the U.S.A. or Canada.

There are also a number of crewed charter yachts that offer 'full-service' cruising, with full crew and all meals provided and served on board to the pampered guests. Most of these vessels are individually owned and operated, and booked in advance for term charters through charter yacht brokers both in the islands and in other countries such as the U.S.A. and Canada.

The crewed yachts of the B.V.I. belong to an association called the Charter Yacht Society, which annually promotes and organises a Charter Boat Show to display the local yachts to charter yacht brokers who come down to the islands to inspect the boats.

There are a number of boats that offer day-sail charters from various locations on both Tortola and Virgin Gorda. They take land-bound guests to popular snorkelling and swimming sites such as the Baths on Virgin Gorda and the caves on Norman Island, returning them to their hotel the same day. Bookings can be made individually or through the hotel.

Cruise ships

A Cunard Line cruise ship calls in the islands weekly, tying up for the day at the commercial dock in Road Harbour. This allows time for their passengers either to visit the shops in Road Town, or possibly take a tour of Tortola, or a day sail. Other cruise ships occasionally come through Sir Francis Drake Channel without stopping, and one cruise liner anchors briefly in North Sound. At present, cruise ships do not make a significant contribution to the B.V.I. economy.

Other marine-oriented activities

Scuba-diving is one of the most popular sports in the islands, which is understandable, since only in tropical waters do you find the elements which combine to create coral reef growth. The combination of this coral life, which attracts myriads of colourful reef fish, and the clear waters and rocky shores of the islands creates an underwater world of tremendous variety that both snorkellers and divers love.

Scuba-diving is only for the trained and the skilled, and there are several certified dive establishments that not only provide training for the novice, but conduct daily trips to dive sites, where diving is done under the expert supervision of professionally qualified dive instructors. It is not necessary for divers to bring heavy and cumbersome equipment to the islands, as all this can be rented at reasonable cost. Most of the dive boats will rendezvous with a charter boat at an anchorage in the islands, and take the guests from the charter yacht to a dive site.

Some of the crewed charter yachts also specialise in scuba-dive trips, and carry on board the necessary equipment and instructors for full enjoyment of this sport. There are a number of excellent books that have been written about diving in the Virgin Islands, and provide full information about the many unique dive sites, providing all the equipment.

Sportfishing is a popular sport in the islands. Sportfishing boats are customarily fairly large, fast power-boats, which can handle the larger seas sometimes found outside the perimeter islands, and get quickly to the fishing sites, which can be as much as ten miles out, to the 'drop off' where the big fish lie. There have been some record catches of large marlin off these islands when conditions have been right.

With all this marine activity, business is generated for a significant number of satellite operations to support the large numbers of vessels involved. Aside from the private marinas operated by charter companies solely for their own vessels, there are eight large marinas which offer a broad spectrum of services that include dockage, water, fuel, ice, utilities and easy access to dockside shops, services and maintenance facilities. Six marinas are on Tortola, and two on Virgin Gorda. There are also a number of mini-marinas, many operated by shoreside hotels, where boats may arrange to tie up overnight, enjoy the hotel facilities, and secure necessary supplies such as water, fuel, and ice.

There are four boat-yards with haul-out facilities, three of which have large areas for yacht storage, all providing extensive maintenance services. Throughout the islands you will find such diverse enterprises as chandleries, radio and electronic shops, sail lofts, riggers, sailing and wind-surfing schools, machine-shops, shipwrights, mechanics, underwater video photography, and others — all catering to the yachting community.

Nor does the bareboat charter yacht guest necessarily have to eat all his dinners on the boat. Actually, it is entirely possible to take a ten-day bareboat charter in the B.V.I. and eat in a different island restaurant at a different anchorage each evening of the charter! There are shore-side hotels which are happy to accommodate yacht charterers by reservation after their own hotel guests, and there are many shore-side restaurants, some located on outlying islands, which make a business of serving this segment of tourists. There is even a floating restaurant located in the popular anchorage at the Bight on Norman Island.

Yacht chartering as an industry has had tremendous growth in the last decade throughout the world, and nowhere has that growth been shown more than here in these islands. There is now a magazine which is published in Florida called 'Yacht Vacations', that devotes its entire content to this world-wide industry.

Shopping

Shopping in the B.V.I. is a mixture of a step back into time: in tiny, low-light shops in quaint old buildings on Main Street in Road Town; or in more modern, airy shops found around the perimeter of Wickham's Cay and in the major hotels and marinas of the islands.

The two major streets in Road Town, both with shops, are Front Street, running north-south along the waterfront as its name implies, and a short block inland, Main Street, which parallels Front Street. The newer shopping centres are found on the northern extension of Front Street which follows the perimeter of Wickham's Cay. While the buildings that house these shops are more modern and utilitarian, the older buildings on Main Street have much more charm and character.

Much of the interest of island visitors will be directed towards the work of local craftsmen and artists and their creations. Some of the craftwork throughout the Caribbean shows both African and early Indian influences, which the local craftsman works into many of the hand-made creations found in the shops. Here are some of the things you may find:

Coral creations

This is a particular art form designed and made exclusively in the B.V.I., and is the product of a firm called Carina Collection. A secret process transforms sea coral into pieces of art of natural beauty in statues of pink and white coral, depicting sea life in the islands. These are exquisite, unique, and reasonably priced.

Jewellery

The owner of a Road Town jewellers creates hand-made gold and silver jewellery indigenous to these islands, such as nautical silver pieces in the form of sailboats and anchors, and nautical necklaces, bracelets, and charms in gold. He also creates moulds of shells found in the islands, casting them with the lost

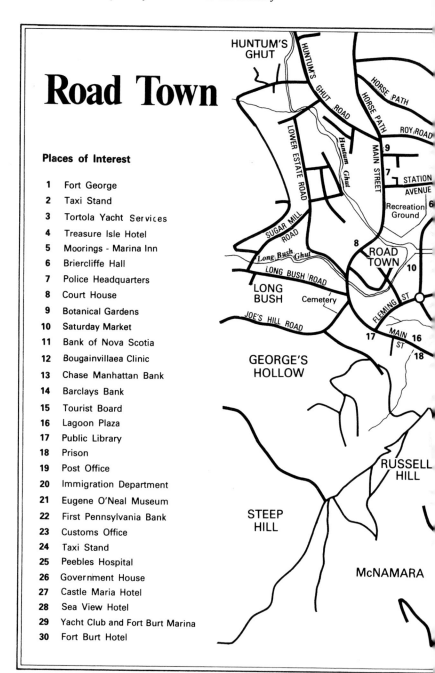

Road Town

Places of Interest

1   Fort George
2   Taxi Stand
3   Tortola Yacht Services
4   Treasure Isle Hotel
5   Moorings - Marina Inn
6   Briercliffe Hall
7   Police Headquarters
8   Court House
9   Botanical Gardens
10   Saturday Market
11   Bank of Nova Scotia
12   Bougainvillaea Clinic
13   Chase Manhattan Bank
14   Barclays Bank
15   Tourist Board
16   Lagoon Plaza
17   Public Library
18   Prison
19   Post Office
20   Immigration Department
21   Eugene O'Neal Museum
22   First Pennsylvania Bank
23   Customs Office
24   Taxi Stand
25   Peebles Hospital
26   Government House
27   Castle Maria Hotel
28   Sea View Hotel
29   Yacht Club and Fort Burt Marina
30   Fort Burt Hotel

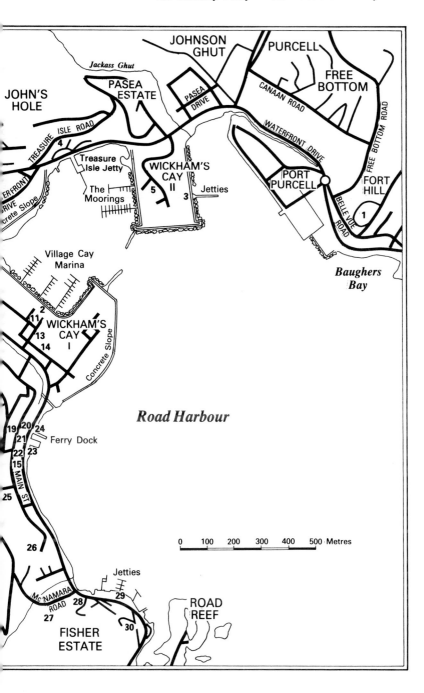

wax process, producing perfect replicas in silver and gold. He also makes charms patterned on local fauna, such as lizards and pelicans.

Silk-screening

Caribbean Handprints is a firm which creates silk-screen fabrics of local design, with patterns such as a map of the B.V.I., turtles, herons, and pelicans, and other designs inspired by the B.V.I.'s fauna and flora. Fabric is sold either by the yard or made up into colourful cotton shirts, dresses, and robes for children and adults. Also produced are such diverse items as tote bags, tea towels, tee-shirts, sarongs, and dolls' dresses — all in Caribbean Handprint fabrics.

Water colours

Island scenes lend themselves perfectly to watercolour sketches, and there are a number of artists here whose works can be found in shops around the islands. Two of the most prominent deserve mention.

Roger Burnett began his roving painting career twenty years ago. He first sailed to the Caribbean in 1974 and since then his vibrant watercolours of the Virgin Islands have been eagerly sought after by collectors. In addition to paintings he has published two illustrated books about the islands and has been commissioned to design many of the island's postage stamps. Studio visits can be arranged by appointment. He has also photographed the island's vernacular architecture and a collection of these photographs can be seen in the Museum on Main Street.

Joseph Hodge is an island-born, self-taught artist who says he 'views his homeland as a giant palette of colour and imagery'. He considers himself primarily a landscape artist, and some of his work also appears in hotels — landscapes painted directly on to the hotel walls. His work is displayed and sold at Collector's Corner, a combination art gallery and collector's shop at Village Cay Marina.

B.V.I. stamps

No shopping trip in Road Town is complete without a stop at the philatelic counter of the main post office on Main Street, or the B.V.I. Philatelic Bureau. B.V.I. stamps are unique, since the stamp's value is stated in U.S. currency, although the Queen's profile or monogram appears on each stamp, along with the issuing country — the British Virgin Islands.

While many countries print stamps for their philatelic value, the B.V.I. has produced its own stamps since 1866. In a little over 100 years, their stamps are enough in demand among collectors to have appreciated substantially in value.

Today, the production of stamps has taken on major importance — the best artists are hired, and the subjects carefully chosen. A total of about 450 different topical designs have been released, mostly with scenes of the islands. There have been issues on birds, butterflies, and ships; on historical figures such as Sir Francis Drake and Columbus; on famous islanders, such

A Roger Burnett water colour depicting local architecture
(*Reproduced by permission of the artist*)

as William Thornton; and on B.V.I. historical events. There was even an issue on rum making. Those interested may write to the B.V.I. Philatelic Society, P.O. Box 704, Road Town, Tortola, B.V.I.

The future of tourism

Few world industries have brighter prospects than tourism. A combination of rising incomes and paid holidays in the developed countries has led to both greater desire and greater ability to travel. Travel costs and travel times have been reduced, and competition among airlines, particularly in the U.S.A., mean costs are likely to be reduced even more. There are more and more 'package deals' where airlines and hotels join to compete for the tourist's pocket-book. As an industry, tourism may be the wave of the future.

Many underdeveloped countries depend on overseas visitors who have the desire to enjoy the attractions provided, and bring the money to spend on them. One of the quickest ways for a country to stifle tourism is to show signs of political instability or lack of welcome. In the Caribbean, both Grenada and Jamaica are examples of how fast tourism wilts when these conditions exist, and how long it takes to revive even when the conditions are removed.

The British Virgin Islands have a record of being one of the most stable governments in the Caribbean, and of warmly welcoming its tourists. Although most of the major tourist-related businesses have been established by non-natives, many island-born residents hold positions of varying responsibility throughout the industry. Both the ex-patriot employers and the island employees have demonstrated the ability to work well together, both recognising that no industry is more service-oriented than tourism, and that a friendly attitude is the catalyst that makes visitors return time after time.

One of the bonuses of a well-established tourist industry is that the satisfied transient tourist of today frequently becomes the vacation home-owner of tomorrow, returning year after year for longer and longer periods, and spending money all year around for staff to service and maintain his vacation home.

One of the principal problems of the tourist industry in the Caribbean has been the relatively short season. There is some success in changing this by intelligent publicity and promotion. Actually, summer in the Caribbean can be very pleasant, particularly in those islands exposed to the trade winds — the B.V.I. being an excellent example of islands that meet these conditions. Reduced summer rates, less crowded facilities, and increased travel from groups and conventions seeking travel bargains are factors that are helping year-round occupancy to grow.

At present the tourist trade in the B.V.I. is predominantly from the U.S.A. and Canada, and seems likely to continue that way. Distance militates against an extensive European trade, though the air services continue to improve to the Caribbean basin. The B.V.I. already gets a handful of tourists from Puerto Rico and South America. That continent may eventually become a better source of tourists, but this would seem primarily to benefit the Spanish-speaking islands of the Caribbean.

What is the islands' future? The key is whether or not an island group can achieve continuing economic success based primarily on tourism — and the answer seems to be positive in the light of the experience of a similar British territory. Bermuda provides an example of a successful economy resting solely on tourism. Many of the conditions in Bermuda have a parallel in the B.V.I. Fresh water in Bermuda must be caught from rain or distilled from the sea. The lack of good soil in most parts precludes extensive farming. Bermuda has made good use of its limited resources — an attractive climate and a warm sea.

Sensible development at home, combined with skilful and effective promotion abroad in the logical marketing areas, has created a sound and successful tourist industry in both Bermuda and the B.V.I. Political stability and a people who understand and welcome the visitor have insured its continuing success in both countries. So long as these conditions continue to exist, both countries should continue to be successful. The single and sole advantage that Bermuda has over the B.V.I. is a direct air link only two hours from the eastern United States and Canada.

The next chapter has a representative list of the principal tourist and marine-oriented establishments that presently (1988) serve visitors in the B.V.I.

Tourism Statistics

The following figures are excerpts from a booklet prepared by the Statistics Division of the B.V.I. government entitled 'Tourism in the British Virgin Islands — 1985 — A Statistical Analysis.' All figures are for the year 1985, and are the most recent figures available.

Description	Numbers
Holiday visitor arrivals	167,676
a) By sea	105,885
b) By air	61,791
Overnight holiday visitors	126,003
a) At hotels	29,054
b) On charter boats	84,604
c) In rented accommodations	1,698
d) In own accommodation/With friends	10,647
Average length of stay (nights)	7.1
Average age of overnight holiday visitors	39
End of year — No. of hotel rooms	848
End of year — No. of B.V.I. based charter boats	299
Average annual occupancy of hotels (%)	52.4
a) Average occupancy — Dec through May (%)	63.6
b) Average occupancy — June through Nov (%)	41.2
Average annual occupancy of charter boats	N/A

Visitors' total expenditure (US $M)   97.3
  a)   Hotel visitors' expenditure   22.4
  b)   Charter boat visitors' expenditure   71.3

Overnight holiday visitors' place of residence
(%)
a)   United States   70.7
b)   United States Virgin Islands   7.7
c)   Puerto Rico   5.9
d)   Canada   4.4
e)   United Kingdom   2.9
f)   Other Caribbean islands   3.9
g)   Other European countries   3.0

11 Tourism Facilities

This chapter provides a representative list of current (1988) establishments that serve tourists in the B.V.I., and a brief description of the services that are offered. It is not intended to be a complete list of all such establishments, nor are any rates quoted. Rates charged by both hotels and charter yacht companies are seasonal, and subject to frequent change. Hotel rates include a 7% hotel tax, and frequently a service charge in lieu of tips and gratuities.

It is recommended that those planning to visit the B.V.I. contact the B.V.I. Tourist Board, which can provide up-to-date

A chartered schooner under sail in Sir Francis Drake Channel
(*Larry and Reba Shepard*)

information on all tourism facilities, and directions for making contact with specific firms.

Those interested in hotel accommodation may also contact a travel agent, while those interested in charter yacht vacations may also contact either a charter yacht broker, a bareboat charter company, or The Charter Yacht Society.

A list of the offices of the B.V.I. Tourist Board and its authorised representatives, with current addresses and telephone numbers at the time of publication, is provided below:

B.V.I. Tourist Board
P.O. Box 134
Road Town, Tortola, B.V.I.
Tel: 809–494–3134
Telex: 7968 VB

B.V.I. Tourist Board
370 Lexington Ave., Suite 511
New York, NY 10017
Tel: 800–835–8530
    212–696–0400
Telex: 669173

B.V.I. Information Office
801 York Mill Rd., Suite 201
Don Mills, Ontario M3B 1X7,
Canada
Tel: 416–443–1859

B.V.I. Information Office
1686 Union Street
San Francisco, CA 94123
Tel: 415–775–0344
    800–922–4873 CA only
    800–922–4874 All other
    states

B.V.I. Tourist Bureau &
  Information Centre
48 Albemarle Street
London W1X 4AR, England
Tel: 01–629–6353

B.V.I. Information Office
Lomerstrasse 28
Hamburg 70, W. Germany
Tel: 4940–695–8846

B.V.I. Information Office
26 Hockerill Street
Bishop's Stortford
Herts CM23 2DW
Tel: 0279–504747

Hotels

The hotels of the B.V.I. have all been constructed since about 1965, and are therefore relatively modern; the rooms reflect this fact. All accommodations listed have private bath, many have open patios or decks. Some are suites, some have kitchenettes. Not all hotels qualify for the prefix 'resort'. Those that do are identified below. All of the islands' 'resort hotels' start with two essential ingredients: beauty and seclusion. Each hotel then adds its own mix of amenities and services.

NAME	*ROOMS*	*PLAN*	*LOCATION*
Biras Creek Hotel	32	**AP**	**North Sound, Virgin Gorda**

Attractive small resort hotel located on 150 acres overlooking both North Sound and the Caribbean Sea. Several beaches, seawater pool, watersports, tennis, nature trails, launch service. Small marina. Restaurant and bar with excellent cuisine. Dinner dress code. Expensive.

| **Bitter End Yacht Club** | 84 | **AP** | **North Sound, Virgin Gorda** |

Combination resort hotel and yacht club, sailing oriented. A 'must see' for visiting yachtsmen. Hillside villas, chalets and rooms are strategically placed around an extensive beach and water frontage facing North Sound. Watersports, sailboats, underwater tours, freshwater pool. Two restaurants and bars, quality cuisine, dinner dress code. Marina facilities and moorings. Shops, conference centre. Ferry service to Beef Island. Expensive.

| **B.V.I. Aquatic Hotel** | 14 | **EP** | **West End, Tortola** |

Overlooking Soper's Hole, walking distance from West End ferry dock. Watersports. Restaurant and bar. Reasonable.

| **Cane Garden Bay Beach Hotel** | 27 | **EP** | **Cane Garden Bay, Tortola** |

On one of Tortola's most beautiful beaches on the North coast. Modest rooms, some with view. Watersports, shops, restaurant and beach bar. Moorings available. Reasonable.

The Castle Maria 32   **EP**   **Road Town,**
Hotel   **Tortola**
Hillside hotel close to Road Town overlooking Road Harbour. Modest rooms, some with kitchenette. Freshwater pool. Restaurant and bar. Reasonable.

CSY Yacht Club 8   **EP**   **Baugher's Bay,**
    Tortola
Charter yacht guests have priority. Rooms overlook Caribbean Sailing Yachts docks and Road Harbour. Restaurant and bar. Reasonable.

Drake's Anchorage 12   **AP**   **North Sound,**
Resort   **Moskito Island**
On 125-acre private island. Cottages and villas overlook North Sound. Several secluded beaches. Watersports, tennis, horseback riding, bicycling. Launch service. Restaurant and beach bar. Moorings available. Expensive.

Fischer's Cove 20   **EP**   **The Valley,**
Beach Hotel   **&MAP**   **Virgin Gorda**
Beachfront rooms and cottages face Sir Francis Drake Channel. Some kitchens. Watersports. Restaurant and bar. Moderate.

Fort Burt Hotel 7   **EP**   **Road Town,**
    Tortola
Hillside hotel with view of Sir Francis Drake Channel. Freshwater pool, sports club, launch service to beach. Restaurant, bar, and disco. Moderate.

Little Dix Bay 84   **AP**   **Little Dix Bay,**
Hotel   **Virgin Gorda**
A Rockresort. First resort hotel in the islands and still one of the best. Rooms and suites encircle beach. Watersports, tennis, horseback riding, bicycles, sailboats. Restaurant and bar. Excellent cuisine. Dinner dress code. Expensive.

Long Bay Hotel   37   **EP**   **Long Bay, Tortola**
Rooms and cottages overlook beach and ocean on Tortola's north shore. Kitchenettes. Pool. Watersports, tennis, pitch-putt golf. Restaurant and beach bar. Reasonable.

Maria's By The Sea 11   **EP**   **Road Town, Tortola**
Overlooks Road Harbour, close to downtown shops. Kitchenettes. Freshwater pool. Launch service to beach. Restaurant and bar. Reasonable.

Marina Cay Hotel   8   **AP**   **Marina Cay**
This small historic hotel, located on a 6-acre islet off Beef Island, has been completely refurbished and recently reopened. Restaurant and beach bar. Watersports. Moorings available. Launch service. Expensive.

Moorings-Mariner   40   **EP**   **Wickham's Cay II, Tortola**
Inn
Charter yacht guests have priority. Rooms with kitchenettes overlook Moorings marina. Freshwater pool, tennis. Restaurant and bar. Moderate.

Nanny Cay Hotel   40   **EP**   **Tortola**
New in 1988, suites with kitchenettes and mini-bars surround a courtyard. Convenient to Nanny Cay marina facilities. Watersports. Freshwater pool. Cable TV. Two restaurants nearby. Expensive.

Ocean View Hotel   12   **EP**   **The Valley, Virgin Gorda**
Overlooks Drake Channel, near Virgin Gorda Yacht Harbour. Restaurant and bar. Reasonable.

Olde Yarde Inn   11   **MAP**   **The Valley, Virgin Gorda**
Quiet garden setting in the valley, close to everything. Library. Restaurant and bar. Fine cuisine. Moderate.

Peter Island Hotel 52   **AP**   Sprat Bay,
Peter Island

An exclusive resort hotel, surrounded by over 1,000 acres. Rooms face Drake Channel and Sprat Bay marina. New suites on beach at Deadman's Bay. Seawater pool. Watersports, tennis, sailboats, bicycles, trails. Frequent ferry to Tortola. Restaurant, bar and beach bar. Excellent cuisine. Dinner dress code. Expensive.

Prospect Reef 131   **EP**   Prospect Reef,
Hotel   Tortola

The islands' largest resort hotel. Rooms and suites face lagoon and Drake Channel. Some kitchenettes. Two freshwater pools, seaside pools, and beach. Small marina. Watersports, tennis, pitch-putt golf. Conference centre. Shops. Restaurant, snack bar, bar, and beach bar. Expensive.

Anegada Reef 12   **AP**   Anegada
Hotel

Small hotel on remote island. Rooms overlook beach. Sportfishing oriented. Watersports. Deep sea and in-shore fishing packages. Restaurant and bar, speciality is barbecued fresh island lobster and fish. Moorings available. Moderate.

Sea View Hotel 20   **EP**   Road Town,
Tortola

Hillside hotel overlooking Road Harbour, walking distance to downtown. Pool. Restaurant and bar. Reasonable.

Sebastians On The 29   **EP**   Little Apple Bay,
Beach   Tortola

Courtyard and beach rooms on secluded north shore beach. Watersports. Restaurant and beach bar. Fine cuisine. Reasonable.

Smuggler's Cove 7   **EP**   South Shore,
Hotel   Tortola

Rooms with kitchenettes on secluded beach, houses on hillside. Watersports. Restaurant and beach bar. Moderate.

Sugar Mill Hotel   21   EP   Apple Bay, Tortola
Suites, cottages, and rooms with kitchenettes, in a garden
setting around a 300-year-old converted sugar mill. All on
north shore beach. Freshwater pool. Watersports. Restaurant, bar, and beach bar. Outstanding cuisine. Dinner
dress code. Moderate.

Tamarind Country 4   EP   Josiah's Bay,
Club Hotel   Tortola
New apartment-type units near secluded beach. Watersports.
Freshwater pool. Restaurant and bar. Reasonable.

Treasure Isle   40   EP   Wickham's Cay,
Hotel   Tortola
Located on side hill overlooking Road Harbour, convenient
to Road Town. Freshwater pool. Tennis. Marina. Nominal
charge for trip to private beach club on Cooper Island.
Restaurant and bar. Fine cuisine. Moderate.

Village Cay Resort 13   EP   Wickham's Cay I,
Marina   Tortola
Regular and 'bunk-style' rooms overlooking the marina
docks and Road Harbour. Convenient to both marina and
downtown shops and facilities. Two restaurants and bar.
Reasonable.

Cottages, Condominiums, and Villas

There are a number of vacation complexes in the B.V.I. ranging from small housekeeping cottages to large villas and homes
with full maid service, each grouped together under common
management, and sometimes labelled as 'vacation homes'.
Some have community dining facilities, making them similar to
hotel operations, some do not. Some are on secluded islands,
which brings them into the category of 'hideaways'. Below is a
representative list of these. Again, the list is not complete, and
no rates are quoted. In general, prices are moderate for small
cottages, expensive for large villas and homes.

NAME	NO. OF UNITS	PLAN	LOCATION
The Cliff Houses	20	**EP**	**Little Apple Bay, Tortola**

Fully equipped housekeeping cottages on cliff above beach on north shore.

Diamond Beach Club	14	**EP**	**Diamond Beach, Virgin Gorda**

Two and three bedroom villas, full kitchen, each over 1,000 square feet, on secluded beach, overlooking Drake Channel. Watersports.

Fort Recovery Estates	10	**EP**	**South Shore, Tortola**

One and two bedroom villas on beach facing Drake Channel. Watersports.

Frenchman's Cay Hotel	11	**EP**	**Frenchman's Cay, Tortola**

New one and two bedroom villas, with livingroom, dining room, kitchen, terrace, on hillside overlooking Drake Channel. Freshwater pool, Tennis court, small beach. Watersports. Restaurant and bar.

Long Bay's peaceful beach on Tortola's north shore   (*B.V.I. Tourist Board*)

Guana Island Club   15   AP   Guana Island
Hillside cottages on 850-acre private island. Six beaches.
Watersports, tennis, pitch-putt golf, trails, croquet, library.
Gracious dining for guests only.

Guavaberry Spring   16   EP   The Valley,
Bay   Virgin Gorda
One and two bedroom vacation homes sited among boulders
and trees, giving both privacy and a view of Drake Channel.
All have living, dining, cooking facilities and patios. Walk
to beach. Watersports.

Josiah's Bay   10   EP   Josiah's Bay,
Cottages   Tortola
Fully equipped housekeeping cottages on secluded beach on
north shore. Watersports.

Leverick Bay,   21   EP   North Sound,
B.V.I. Villa   Virgin Gorda
Two bedroom condominiums, two and three bedroom houses
on hillside with view of North Sound. Two beaches, freshwater pool. Marina. Watersports, sailboats. Restaurant and
beach bar.

Necker Island   20   AP   North Sound,
**   Virgin Gorda**
A private island with a large de luxe mansion accommodat-
ing from 10 to 20 guests. Can be rented only in its entirety.
Several beaches, freshwater pool, watersports, exercise faci-
lities, full services, complete privacy. Very expensive.

Sandy Ground   8   EP   Jost Van Dyke
One to three bedroom houses on secluded estate with private
beach. Watersports.

In addition to the hotels, cottages, villas and houses listed
above, there are a large number of small properties comprising
everything from single rooms to large homes, including small

hotels, guest houses, apartments, even campgrounds, that regularly rented to visitors. For full information, contact the B.V.I. Tourist Board.

When visitors arrive in the islands, we suggest they pick up a copy of *The Welcome Tourist Guide*, a bi-monthly magazine published in the islands in collaboration with the B.V.I. Tourist Board and the Hotel and Commerce Association. This informative and well-written magazine is available free at most tourist establishments. It contains interesting articles about the islands, lists of tourist facilities, and facts about the islands, along with numerous advertisements by local firms.

Restaurants

Island restaurants are justly proud of both their food and service. A great many are located in hotels, and while seating priority is normally given to hotel guests, almost all are open to non-guests. Shoreside hotels cater to yacht charterers as well as their own guests, usually requiring advance reservations, some with dinner dress codes. Hotel dining facilities have already been covered in the list of hotels given above.

There are a number of restaurants that are not a part of hotel complexes, and which make a special point of catering to both yacht charterers looking for a place to dine ashore, and to land-based visitors looking for an alternate place to dine. A sample follows — it is not intended as a complete list — with their locations, and a brief description of each.

In addition to those listed, there are a number of other island restaurants, some specialising in local foods, which have developed a strong local following, and are worth seeking out.

No attempt is made here to rate restaurants — we leave that to the experts. Those interested in restaurant ratings are referred to *Fielding's Caribbean Guide*.

NAME	LOCATION
The Apple	**Little Apple Bay, Tortola**

Authentic West Indian restaurant, specialising in local seafood served in an intimate atmosphere. Reservations required.

The Bath & Turtle — The Valley, Virgin Gorda

Located in the Virgin Gorda Yacht Habour shopping centre, overlooking fountains and gardens. English pub, serving liquor and food at modest prices.

Brandywine Bay Restaurant — Brandywine Bay, Tortola

Fine food presented on a cobblestone garden terrace of a secluded private estate overlooking Drake Channel. Reservations requested.

The Captain's Table — Wickham's Cay I, Tortola

A newcomer, located behind Village Cay Marina, which promises a French flavour in its food, its drinks, and its French/Caribbean atmosphere.

Carib Casseroles — Road Town, Tortola

A small garden restaurant overlooking Main Street that serves a wide variety of West Indian and international specialties. Dinner reservations requested.

Carib Casseroles is housed in a charming old building on Main Street, Road Town   (*Michael Bourne*)

Chez Michelle Restaurant **The Valley, Virgin Gorda**
Food prepared by creative chef, served in lamp-lit surroundings of custom wood and stone work. Reservations requested.

The Cloud Room **Road Town, Tortola**
Their driver picks you up at your Road Harbour location and drives you to a hilltop restaurant which has a magnificent view of the harbour and Drake Channel. Quality food, nicely presented. Price includes food, wine and transportation. Reservations required.

Cooper Island Beach Club **Manchineel Bay, Cooper Island**
A small restaurant and bar under the palm trees, with a relaxed and casual atmosphere serving good food and drinks. Moorings available. Dinner reservations requested.

Elena's **Road Town, Tortola**
A popular luncheon spot on Front Street. Conveniently located close to ferry dock and shopping. Local foods a speciality.

The Last Resort **Trellis Bay, Beef Island**
Good basic English fare, home-made soups, roast beef and Yorkshire pudding buffet. Entertainment by Tony Snell is the main attraction after dinner. Seasonal. Reservations required.

Mrs Scatliffe's **Carrot Bay, Tortola**
Home-like atmosphere with friendly personal attention marks this family-run restaurant. 100% native fare from papaya soup to soursop sherbet. Softly played island music adds ambience. Reservations required.

Neptune's Treasure **Anegada**
A seaside restaurant in walking distance from the anchorage at Anegada's West End. Fresh caught fish and lobster a speciality. Home-like and casual.

Peg Leg Landing   **Nanny Cay, Tortola**
Waterside pub and restaurant at Nanny Cay Marina. New menu and management promises first class food and service at medium class prices. Relaxed and casual.

The Pub   **Road Harbour, Tortola**
Longtime yachtsmen's hangout at Fort Burt Marina, with speciality dish each night. Moderately priced food has always been consistently well prepared here. Casual.

The Pusser's Landing   **Frenchman's Cay, Tortola**
Old Royal Navy artefacts adorn this casual waterside pub and restaurant, where speciality drinks are concocted from Pusser's Rum, and food is a mixture of English and island fare. Reservations not necessary.

Skyworld   **Mountain Top, Tortola**
Panoramic view of all the Virgin Islands makes this a popular spot both for luncheon and for sunset dinners. Fine food from hamburgers to six-course dinners with daily specials keep people coming back.

The Virgin Queen   **Road Town, Tortola**
Tiffany lamps and hand-carved wood decor offer a warm atmosphere, complemented by interesting European dishes at dinner. Homemade pizza is a luncheon speciality. Conveniently located to both downtown and Wickham's Cay.

The Wharf & Mr Fish   **Wickham's Cay I, Tortola**
These adjoining restaurants behind Village Cay Marina, one outdoors, one indoors, specialise in seafood and fast food fish dishes. Daily specialities come with a West Indian emphasis.

The William Thornton   **The Bight, Norman Island**
This is the Virgin Island's only floating restaurant, a Baltic

Trader, redone to look like an ancient galleon, anchored in the bight. Good basic food from hamburgers to barbecued chicken served in an atmosphere that is really laid back. A yachtsman's delight.

Bareboat charter yacht companies

Bareboat yacht chartering is one of the major tourist industries in the B.V.I. This segment of the industry is dominated by a relatively small group of companies which operate fleets of sailboats, each offering a wide variety of choices to prospective charterers. All operate from marinas in the islands, some have adjacent hotels to provide land-based accommodations for their guests prior to, or at the conclusion of, their yacht charter trip. Charter yacht companies will work through travel agents, but prefer to deal directly with the client, and therefore maintain

Brightly coloured spinnakers are a common sight on charter yachts (*Larry and Reba Shepard*)

sales and reservations offices in the U.S.A. or Canada. Listed below are the current bareboat companies operating from bases in the B.V.I., their location in the B.V.I., and their current sales office address and telephone number.

NAME   *B.V.I. LOCATION*

Caribbean Sailing Yachts, Ltd   **Baugher's Bay, Tortola**
  Sales Office: P.O. Box 491, Tenafly, NJ 07670 U.S.A.
  Tel: 201-568-0390/800-631-1593

Cruising Centre Charters   **Village Cay Marina,**
                                       Tortola
  Sales Office: 913 Meyer St., Seabrook, TX 77586 U.S.A.
  Tel: 713-474-5481/800-231-4628

Go Vacations Limited   **Fat Hog's Bay, Tortola**
  Sales Office: 129 Carlingview Dr., Rexdale, Ontario M9W
  5E7 Canada   Tel: 416-674-1880/800-387-3998

The Moorings, Ltd   **Wickham's Cay II,**
                                       Tortola
  Sales Office: 1305 US 19 South, Suite 402, Clearwater,
  FL 33546. U.S.A.   Tel: 813-535-1446/800-535-7289

North-South Yacht Charters, Ltd   **Leverick Bay,**
                                       North Sound
                                       Virgin Gorda
  Sales Office: P.O. Box 59, Buffalo, NY 14205 U.S.A.   Tel:
  800-387-4964

Stevens Yachts, Inc   **Frenchmen's Cay,**
                                       Tortola
  Sales Office: 252 East Ave., East Norwalk, CT 06855
  U.S.A.   Tel: 203-866-8989/800-638-7044

Tortola Marine Management, Ltd   **Nanny Cay Marina,**
                                       Tortola
  Sales Office: 47 Telegraph St., South Boston, MA 02127
  U.S.A.   Tel: 617-269-0240/800-633-0155

Tortola Yacht Charters   **Nanny Cay Marina,**
                                   Tortola
Sales Office: 5825 Sunset Drive, Suite 206, South Miami,
FL 33143 U.S.A.   Tel: 305–665–1217/800–243–9936
Tel: 800–824–1844

Tropic Island Yacht Management **Treasure Isle Jetty,**
                                    Tortola
Sales Office: 449A Jarvis St., Toronto, Ontario M4Y 2H2
Canada   Tel: 416–925–6763

Virgin Islands Trawler Charters **Nanny Cay Marina,**
                                     Tortola
Sales Office: P.O. Box 595, Lenox Hill Sta., New York,
NY 10021. U.S.A.   Tel: 212–744–0438

West Indies Yacht Charters   **Maya Cove, Tortola**
Sales Office: 2190 S.E. 17 St Suite 203, Ft. Lauderdale,
FL 33316 U.S.A.   Tel: 304–525–4123/800–327–2290

Crewed yacht charters

While some bareboat charter yacht companies offer crewed
yacht charters, most crewed charter yachts based in the B.V.I.
are individually owned. There are currently about 100 such
yachts offering term charters, all by prior reservation. Full
information regarding size of vessel, amenities and services
offered, and rates, may be obtained from charter yacht brokers.
Most B.V.I. based crewed charter yachts belong to the Charter
Yacht Society, and a list of both boats and brokers may be
obtained by writing to:

The Charter Yacht Society of the B.V.I.
P.O. Box 6039, Road Town, Tortola, B.V.I.
Tel: 809–494–3174 or 494–2845

Additional information may be secured on the subject of both
bareboat and crewed yacht chartering from 'Yacht Vacations',
which is the only magazine that is solely devoted to covering

the field of charter yacht vacations. The magazine can be found on most major news-stands, or by subscription from:

'Yacht Vacations'
P.O. Box 755
Jensen Beach, FL 33457–0755
Tel: 305–334–2003

Scuba-diving companies

Scuba-diving is an important watersport in the clear, tropical waters around the islands, and there are many fine dive sites to be explored by *aficionados*. The companies listed below all offer full services for the enjoyment of the sport, including equipment sales and rentals, training and instruction, airfills, dive tours, rendezvous dives, and operate specially equipped dive boats manned by certificated personnel. In addition to the companies listed, some of the crewed charter yachts (see above) are also equipped to offer scuba-diving vacations. For full information, contact The B.V.I. Tourist Board or:

B.V.I. Dive Operators Association
P.O. Box 13, Road Town, Tortola, B.V.I.
Tel: 809–494–3235

NAME	LOCATION
Baskin in the Sun	Propect Reef Marina, Tortola Treasure Isle Jetty, Tortola
Blue Water Divers	Nanny Cay Marina, Tortola
Dive B.V.I., Ltd.	Virgin Gorda Yacht Harbour

Kilbride's Underwater Tours   North Sound, Virgin
Gorda

Underwater Safaris   Wickham's Cay II,
Tortola

Yacht marinas

The large number of boats, both B.V.I. based and visiting boats
from nearby islands, that constantly ply the waters of the
B.V.I., occasionally need a place to dock — to re-coup, re-
supply, and re-provision. To met this need, the B.V.I. has a
good number of strategically placed marinas. We have broken
this group into two classifications — the large, full-fledged
marina; and the mini-marina, with limited dock space. Following is the list of these facilities, their locations, and a brief
description of services provided.

Marinas

NAME   *LOCATION*

The Bitter End Yacht Club   North Sound, Virgin
Gorda

Docks for 18 boats plus 50 moorings. Ice, water, 110v/220v
electricity, dinghy gas. Restrooms and showers. Beach. Bar
and restaurant, dinner reservations.

Fort Burt Marina   Road Harbour, Tortola

Overnight or permanent slips. Ice, water, fuel, 110v electricity Restrooms and showers. Chandlery and provisions. Bar
and restaurant. Close to Road Town.

Inner Harbour Marina   Wickham's Cay I,
Tortola

A single dock with finger piers along the east jetty south of
Village Cay Marina. Water, ice, duty free fuel. Telephones
and cable TV. Convenient to Road Town shops.

The Moorings   **Wickham's Cay II,**
                                    Tortola

Dockage for 90 boats. Ice, water, fuel, 110v/220v electricity.
Restrooms and showers. Bar and restaurant, freshwater pool,
tennis. Close to chandlery, provisions, marine repair facilities.

Nanny Cay Marine Centre   **Nanny Cay, Tortola**

Dockage for 180 boats. Ice, water, fuel, 110v/220v electricity.
Restrooms and showers. Bar and restaurant, snack bar. Provisions, shops, laundry, maintenance and repair facilities.

Treasure Isle Marina & Jetty   **Wickham's Cay, Tortola**

Ice, water, 110v electricity. Restrooms and showers. Bar and
restaurant. Freshwater pool. Marine supplies.

Village Cay Resort Marina   **Wickham's Cay I,**
                                    Tortola

Dockage for 106 boats. Ice, water, 110v/220v electricity.
Cable TV. Bar and restaurant, shops, provisions, close to
downtown.

Virgin Gorda Yacht Harbour   **The Valley, Virgin Gorda**

Dockage for 120 boats. Ice, water, fuel, 110v/220v electricity. Restrooms and showers. Bar and restaurant. Shops, provisions, maintenance and repair facilities.

Mini-Marinas

NAME   *LOCATION*

Biras Creek   **North Sound, Virgin**
                                    Gorda

Dockage for 10 boats. Water, fuel, 110v/220v electricity.
Restrooms and showers. Bar and restaurant, dinner reservations.

Safely anchored for the night   (*Larry and Reba Shepard*)

Leverick Bay   **North Sound, Virgin
                                    Gorda**

Ice, water, fuel, 110v electricity. Restrooms and showers. Bar
and restaurant. Freshwater pool.

Peter Island Yacht Harbour   **Sprat Bay, Peter Island**

Ice, water, fuel, 110v/220v electricity. Restrooms and showers. Bar and restaurant, dinner reservations.

Prospect Reef Resort Harbour   **Prospect Reef, Tortola**

Ice, water, fuel, 110v electricity. Restrooms and showers. Bar
and restaurant, shops.

Stevens Yachts   **Frenchman's Cay,
                                    Tortola**

Ice, water, fuel, 110v electricity. Restrooms, bar and restaurant. Moorings available.

West Indies Yacht Charters   **Maya Cove, Tortola**

Ice, water, fuel. Restrooms and showers. Bar and restaurant.

In addition to the marine facilities listed here, there are a
number of other water-oriented services offered in the islands,
such as day-sails, sportfishing boats, sailing schools, boardsailing
schools and rentals, boatyards and slipways. For information,
contact the B.V.I. Tourist Board or see *The Welcome Tourist
Guide* after your arrival in the islands.

12 Selected Sources Consulted

Books — History and Government

Abrahams, Roger D. and Szwed, John F., eds. *After Africa, Extracts from British Travel Accounts and Journals of the Seventeenth, Eighteenth, and Nineteenth Centuries Concerning the Slaves, their Manners, and Customs in the British West Indies.* New Haven and London: Yale University Press, n.d.

Andrews, Kenneth R., ed. *The Last Voyage of Drake & Hawkins.* Cambridge: Published for the Hakluyt Society at the University Press, 1972.

Boyer, William W. *America's Virgin Islands, A History of Human Rights and Wrongs.* Durham, NC: Carolina Academic Press, n.d.

Coke, Thomas, LL.D. *A History of the West Indies, Vol. III.* London: Printed for the Author, 1811.

Dookhan, Isaac. *A History of the British Virgin Islands: Some Notes on its Writing and Bibliography.* n.p. 1967.

Goveia, Elsa V. *Slave Society in the British Leeward Islands at the End of the Eighteenth Century.* New Haven and London: Yale University Press, 1965.

Higman, B. W. *Slave Populations of the British Caribbean, 1807–1834.* Baltimore and London: The Johns Hopkins University Press, n.d.

Jenkins, Charles F. *Tortola, A Quaker Experiment of Long Ago in the Tropics.* London: Friends' Bookshop, 1923.

Lewis, Gordon K. *The Virgin Islands, A Caribbean Lilliput.* Evanston, IL: Northwestern University Press, 1972.

Lowenthal, David. *West Indian Societies.* London, New York, Toronto: Oxford University Press, 1972.

Mitchell, Sir Harold, Bt. Dr. e's sc. pol. *Caribbean Patterns, A Political and Economic Study of the Contemporary Caribbean, Second Edition.* New York & Toronto: John Wiley & Sons, n.d.

Pitman, Frank Wesley. *The Development of the British West Indies, 1700–1763.* n.p.: Archon Books, 1967.

Ragatz, Lowell Joseph, Ph.D. *The Fall of the Planter Class in the Caribbean, 1763–1833.* New York: Octagon Books, 1971.

Books — Miscellaneous subjects

Allen, Robert Porter. *Birds of the Caribbean.* New York: The Viking Press, 1961.

Bond, James. *Birds of the West Indies.* Boston: Houghton Mifflin Co., 1961.

The Caribbean Year Book, (various years). Toronto: Caribook Limited, annual.

Glanville, Gail and Jenik, Armando. *Diving Guide to the U.S. and British Virgin Islands.* Miami: Argos, Inc., n.d.

Hayes, Elizabeth S. *Spices and Herbs Lore & Cookery.* New York: Dover Publications, Inc., 1961.

Honychurch, Penelope N. *Caribbean Wild Plants & their Uses.* London and Basingstoke: Macmillan Caribbean, 1986.

Lee, Sidney, ed. *Dictionary of National Biography, Vol. XXXIII.* London: Smith, Elder & Co., 15 Waterloo Pl., 1893.

Lewisohn, Florence. *Tales of Tortola and the British Virgin Islands.* n.p.: Published by the Author, Revised Edition, 1981.

Maycock, James Dottin, MD, FL.S. *Catalogue of Plants, Indigenous, Naturalized, and Cultivated in the British West India Colonies.* London: James W. Parker, West Strand, n.d.

Shepard, Reba E. *The Banana Cookbook.* London and Basingstoke: Macmillan Caribbean, 1986.

Shepard, Reba E. *The Charter Cookbook.* London and Basingstoke: Macmillan Caribbean, 1985.

Springer, Rita G. *Caribbean Cookbook.* London: Pan Books,

Ltd., 1975.

West Indies Pilot, Vol. II. London: Published by the Hydrographer of the Navy, Eleventh Edition, 1969.

Booklets

The B.V.I. Yacht Club, 1987 Yearbook. Road Town: The B.V.I. Yacht Club, Box 200, Annual.

Government of the B.V.I. *British Virgin Islands, Report for the Years 1963 and 1964*. London: Her Majesty's Stationery Office, 1966.

A Guide to Historic Places in the British Virgin Islands. Road Town: Hotel and Tourist Association, 1979.

Pickering, Vernon W., ed. *The B.V.I. Tourist Handbook 1986*. n.p.: Laurel Publications International, 1986.

Tourism in the British Virgin Islands 1985, A Statistical Analysis No. 12. Road Town: Statistics Division, Planning Unit, Chief Minister's Office, 1986.

White, Mary (text) and Clarke, Natalie (graphics). *Cane Garden Bay*. Road Town: B.V.I. National Parks Trust and Government of the B.V.I., n.d.

Newspapers and Periodicals

Abbott, Linnell M., ed. *The BVI Beacon*. Road Town: n.p., P.O. Box 830, 1x-weekly.

Abbott-Smith, Michelle, ed. *Resource* (Jan.–Mar. 1986). Road Town: Aaronsrod Communications, Ltd., Quarterly.

Backshall, Paul, ed. *The Welcome Tourist Guide*. Road Town: Island Publishing Services, Ltd., Bi-monthly.

Caribbean Insight, 9:5 (May, 1986). London: West India Committee, Box 100, 48 Albemarle St., Monthly.

Caribbean Travel Directory, 1983–84. Grand Cayman: Caribbean Publishing Co. with Caribbean Hotel Association, Annual.

Downing, Carlos, ed. *The Island Sun*. Road Town: Sun Enterprizes (B.V.I.) Ltd., Box 21, 2x-weekly.

Image — The Newsletter of the B.V.I. Tourist Board (July–August

1986). Road Town: B.V.I. Tourist Board, Bi-monthly.

Marine Scene (a supplement of *The Daily News*). Charlotte Amalie, U.S.V.I.: Gannett Publishing Co., Monthly.

Moll, V. P., ed. *Virgin Islands Historical Documents*, 2:1 (March–April, 1985). Tortola: n.p., Bi-monthly.

North Soundings, Chicago: The Bitter End Yacht Club, 875 N. Michigan Ave , Quarterly.

Shepard, Michael L., ed. *Yacht Vacations*, (March, 1987). Jensen Beach, FL: Robert H. Rogers, Box 755, Monthly.